the anti-anxiety diet cookbook

stress-free recipes
to mellow your mood

Ali Miller, RD, LD, CDE

ULYSSES PRESS

Published in the United States by:
ULYSSES PRESS
P.O. Box 3440
Berkeley, CA 94703
www.ulyssespress.com

ISBN: 978-1-61243-935-8
Library of Congress Control Number: 2019905571

Printed in the United States by Versa Press
10 9 8 7 6 5 4 3 2 1

Acquisitions editor: Bridget Thoreson
Managing editor: Claire Chun
Editor: Renee Rutledge
Proofreader: Jessica Benner
Front cover design: Rebecca Lown
Interior design: what!design @ whatweb.com
Photographs: © Becki Yoo

NOTE TO READERS: This book has been written and published strictly for informational and educational purposes only. It is not intended to serve as medical advice or to be any form of medical treatment. You should always consult your physician before altering or changing any aspect of your medical treatment and/or undertaking a diet regimen, including the guidelines as described in this book. Do not stop or change any prescription medications without the guidance and advice of your physician. Any use of the information in this book is made on the reader's good judgment after consulting with his or her physician and is the reader's sole responsibility. This book is not intended to diagnose or treat any medical condition and is not a substitute for a physician.

This book is independently authored and published and no sponsorship or endorsement of this book by, and no affiliation with, any trademarked brands or other products mentioned within is claimed or suggested. All trademarks that appear in ingredient lists and elsewhere in this book belong to their respective owners and are used here for informational purposes only. The author and publisher encourage readers to patronize the quality brands mentioned and pictured in this book.

Contents

Introduction

The foods we eat play a dynamic role, both good and bad, in our brain chemistry. In fact, foods can regulate mood, emotions, and brain-signaling pathways. Some things, such as chocolate and spicy peppers, even have psychoactive compounds. This book's purpose is to provide you with recipes to support regulation of stress signals and promote a mellow, grounded mental state. When the brain is running on a high-octane fuel of ketones supported by essential nutritional compounds without inflammatory distraction, brain chemistry and mood stability have a reciprocal relationship for favorable, whole-body physiology.

The foods you select can function as drivers of deficiency or building blocks for restoration. This book provides recipes to nourish your body while satiating cravings and supporting your brain signaling.

During times of anxiety, we are more likely to overindulge in sugary or processed, hyper-palatable foods, creating a dopamine spike to numb our racing mind or shift our thought patterns from restlessness and worry to escape and bliss. However, the dopamine spike from typical go-to snacks laden with refined carbohydrates and chemical ingredients is short-lived. These processed foods can actually leach minerals, deplete B vitamins, and drive blood sugar imbalance, perpetuating mood instability, cravings, and dissatisfaction.

I wrote this book to support the science and strategy of *The Anti-Anxiety Diet,* which teaches you how to thrive rather than simply survive! When you shift to the anti-anxiety diet protocol, you can reduce inflammation, repair gut integrity, and provide an abundance of nutrients that promote enhanced absorption. As you optimize the body's nutritional status and reduce stress signals, the systems that regulate hormones and stress chemicals in both the gut and the fight-or-flight axis are able to downshift from high alert, "always on" chronic anxiety to reacting only in times of need. This creates a more even-keeled mood and mental processing with balanced physical responses, which relaxes the body and gives positive feedback to the mind, telling the body it is safe.

Abundance Is as Powerful as Restriction!

When applying food as medicine, do so with the double-edged sword approach: Focus as much on removing proinflammatory, mood-disturbing ingredients as you do on consuming abundant therapeutic foods to tonify and support the body. Every recipe in this book has two or more ingredients to reduce inflammation, reset microbiome, repair gut lining, restore nutrient deficiencies, rebound adrenals, and balance neurotransmitters. The food-as-medicine introduction to each recipe will enlighten as well as empower you to apply the benefits of the featured ingredients beyond the dish of focus.

Anti-Anxiety Diet Guide

I've compiled some resources and worksheets to accompany this cookbook. You can download this Anti-Anxiety Diet Guide at www.alimillerrd.com/anti-anxiety-diet-guide. Your complementary download includes:

- Building an Anti-Anxiety Diet Pantry
- Elimination Diet Reintroduction
- Exchange List
- Four-Week Meal Plan
- Grocery List
- Meal Planning/Prep Tips
- Mixing Up Lunches and Snacks
- My Favorite Products
- Probiotic Challenge

Chapter 1

Why the Anti-Anxiety Diet?

As a functional medicine practitioner, I take on the role of detective for my patients' bodies, seeking out the cause of their illness or imbalance to uncover their path to healing. In an initial session, I spend over an hour thoroughly getting to know a patient's story, including what triggers and incidents drove them to simply surviving rather than thriving. I approach each client with upstream support, taking proactive measures to regulate and address the factors impacting their body's function.

In the past 10 years of running my clinic, Naturally Nourished, I have observed positive trends in addressing chronic illness, optimal wellness, and weight loss with diet intervention, advanced labs, and targeted supplemental therapy. I became well versed in functional approaches to various systems of the body, addressing leaky gut, dysbiosis or small intestinal bacterial overgrowth (SIBO), hormone imbalance, metabolic syndrome, and inflammatory, neurological, and autoimmune conditions with successful outcomes.

I realized, however, that no matter what condition I am working with, the patient will not heal if the mind and stress response are not sound or balanced. Anxiety and stress response play a vital role in the pathology of many conditions via the hypothalamic-pituitary-adrenal (HPA) axis, which influences the autonomic nervous system—the primary controller of involuntary function in the body. Managing the HPA axis is essential to recovery and optimal health. When the body is in a parasympathetic state (also known as rest and digest), regulatory functions are optimized, including metabolism, digestion, hormones, sleep, and body composition. When the body is in a sympathetic state (also known as fight or flight), reactive functions are expressed, influencing blood sugar, blood pressure, cortisol, adrenaline, inflammation, microbiome, and, ultimately, inducing a chronic state of tension or anxiety.

As discussed in *The Anti-Anxiety Diet*, when the HPA axis is in overdrive mode, you are susceptible to:

- **Dysbiosis/bacterial imbalance.** This can allow for the overgrowth of opportunistic bad bacteria.

- **Leaky gut.** Damage to the gut lining allows larger food particles into the bloodstream, driving inflammatory response, food sensitivity, and, often, autoimmune reactivity.
- **Nutrient deficiency.** The body burns through more nutrients in times of stress response.
- **Adrenal overdrive or insufficiency.** This can lead to elevated blood sugar, blood pressure, weight gain, and chronic fatigue.

The impacts of anxiety and chronic stress extend beyond burnout or emotional imbalance: HPA axis sympathetic overdrive, over time, destroys the body.

What Is the Anti-Anxiety Diet?

The anti-anxiety diet starts with a high-fat low-carb (HFLC) ketogenic diet. This provides an additional mood-stabilizing benefit beyond blood sugar control. (We'll get to this in Chapter 2.)

I developed the anti-anxiety diet as a way to reset multiple bodily processes using my Foundational 6 Rs approach to accelerate mind-body balance and promote optimal health. The food therapy in this book focuses on fueling the body with vitamins, minerals, antioxidants, and amino acids to provide building blocks for neurotransmitters as signals in the brain that help to manage mood, reduce cravings, and resolve anxiety.

The anti-anxiety diet's Foundational 6 Rs are: Remove Inflammatory Foods, Reset Gut Microbiome, Repair GI Lining, Restore Micronutrient Status, Rebound Adrenals, Rebalance Neurotransmitters.

1. Remove Inflammatory Foods

When you consume inflammatory foods, a greater amount of inflammatory chemicals circulate in your bloodstream. These can cross the blood-brain barrier, interfere with the way your neurotransmitters function, and drive distress signals, keeping the body in fight-or-flight mode. The primary inflammatory foods identified in the anti-anxiety diet are gluten, corn, soy, dairy, and sugar. These foods are included for one or many reasons: containing compounds driving gut irritation, the presence of omega-6 proinflammatory fats, the susceptibility to GMO farming practices, residual pesticide treatment, and influence on blood sugar levels.

Beyond these foods driving inflammation, which disturbs mental health and stress response, gluten with gluteomorphin and dairy with casomorphin have a direct relationship with our opioid receptors in the brain that may drive addictive behavior, aggression, and outrage, and worsen mood imbalance.

By removing inflammatory and mood-imbalancing foods, not only will you cool and soothe your GI tract, but your immune system, less burdened by compounds in the bloodstream, will signal your inflammatory army to retreat, reducing aches, pains, fatigue, and insulin resistance while supporting favorable neurotransmitter expression.

What Does This Mean for You?

To remove inflammatory foods, I recommend going on a 12-week elimination diet. This means no gluten, corn, soy, dairy, or sugar (the five inflammatory foods) for 12 or more weeks.

During this period (and beyond for optimal eating on a long-term basis), it is important to be mindful of hidden sources of inflammatory ingredients and carefully read all food labels.

Reduce total carbohydrates to 30 grams max per day to experience nutritional ketosis. This will reduce inflammation quickly and enhance mental clarity. (See Why Keto? on page 22.)

Inflammatory food	Replacement	Recipe inspiration
Gluten/carbs as pasta	Zoodles (zucchini noodles) or other spiralized veggies	Sauté with olive oil and herbs, top with protein and sauce of choice.
Gluten/carbs as pizza crust	Cauliflower crust, almond/coconut flour blend, or spaghetti squash boat	Top with your favorite herbed olive oil, grilled veggies, and meats of choice.
Soy/soy sauce	Coconut liquid aminos	Use soy sauce and coconut liquid aminos 1:1 as dip for sushi or in any stir fry or umami flavor application.
Dairy as a beverage	Coconut milk, almond milk, or any nut milk, unsweetened (look for options free of binders and fillers such as carrageenan and guar gum)	For a boost of selenium, blend 2 cups of Brazil nuts with 5 cups of filtered water, vanilla, salt, and optional raw honey to sweeten.
Vegetable seed oils and industrialized oils	Virgin coconut oil, refined coconut oil*, tallow*, lard*, virgin avocado oil, refined avocado oil*, macadamia nut oil, olive oil *Can be used for high heat application over 350°F	Fats with asterisks can be used in the oven for roasting or in a marinade on a high-heat grill. Choose unrefined or extra-virgin oils to retain the most nutrients at lower heat, such as a light sauté, herbed oil sauce, or salad dressing.
Cheese	Other savory snacks or toppings such as avocado, olives, or nut cheese	nut cheese
Yogurt	Homemade coconut yogurt using a quality probiotic capsule	coconut yogurt

A 12-week elimination diet may sound extreme, but with chronic exposure to these inflammatory foods, many of us operate at a mediocre to poor level, intermittently experiencing undesired symptoms such as anxiety, depression, fatigue, body aches, and digestive distress, and accepting this suboptimal state as aging or the norm; this leaves us unable to detect subtle feedback of dietary reactions. Going from mediocre to crappy doesn't feel significant...but going from absolutely amazing to crappy sure does! Once you commit to eliminating drivers of inflammation and supporting the gut with the anti-anxiety diet, you wring out inflammatory chemicals and shift your body's function from mediocre to amazing. You will feel more aware of what foods your body is sensitive to or intolerant of.

If you are practicing nutritional ketosis, none of the five inflammatory foods are recommended for reintroduction into the diet, with the exception of cultured, raw, A2 dairy (dairy with less inflammatory casein) and fermented soy due to their health-supporting properties. However, it is reasonable to test portions of carbohydrate-containing foods and stay within your desired carbohydrate restriction. For example, you may wish to try flour in a sauce when dining out, but you would not consume a piece of bread. However, even testing in sauce is not necessary, and it would be optimal to stay 100% gluten-free. I recommend it only if you desire the flexibility and knowledge of true reactivity. Instead, avoid testing and opt for a dark chocolate bar at 80% cacao or greater that has minimal cane sugar and keeps you well within your desired carbohydrate range.

To determine which foods work best for your body, use the Elimination Diet Reintroduction worksheet from the Anti-Anxiety Diet Guide at alimillerrd.com/anti-anxiety-diet-guide.

Recipes to Remove Inflammatory Foods

❖ *Anti-Inflammatory Electrolyte Elixir, page 135*

❖ *Golden Lemon Zinger with Coconut Pistachios and Shrimp, page 60*

❖ *Dashi Broth Soup with Seaweed, page 64*

❖ *Crispy Fish Tacos in Cabbage Cups, page 92*

❖ *Pistachio Golden Milk, page 134*

2. Reset Gut Microbiome

Your body has over 100 trillion cells of bacteria and yeast that line the mucosal membranes of your mouth, skin, and gut. Together they comprise 3 to 5 pounds of living bacteria known as the microbiome. The microbiome is the manufacturing plant for neurotransmitters and has the ability to work with your body in a state of symbiosis or against your body in a state of dysbiosis.

In a state of symbiosis, the microbiome produces anti-anxiety neurotransmitters such as serotonin and GABA. It also activates other complex mechanisms to regulate your stress and anxiety response. If the gut is in a dysbiotic state with bad strains of bacteria or yeast, it will produce more stress signals and anxiety-driving neurotransmitters such as epinephrine.

In addition to its influence on the sympathetic and parasympathetic stress response, the gut is the second brain of the body. It has unique signaling via the enteric nervous system, directly communicating with the central nervous system of the brain and spine.

When you are able to get those bugs working for you rather than against you, you may benefit beyond the increase of serotonin and GABA to experience improved regularity, less bloating, and clearer skin.

What Does This Mean for You?

A serving of culture a day keeps the doctor away! Focus on incorporating probiotic-rich foods into your daily diet. As dairy isn't allowed in the first 12 weeks, you will explore coconut yogurt, cultured vegetables, and beverages. Use the A Serving of Culture a Day chart as a guide.

Intolerance to probiotics is an indication of dysbiosis, which can be addressed with a gut cleanse. Search "Ali Miller RD Beat the Bloat Cleanse" for details. If you aren't sure if you tolerate probiotic foods or have a balanced gut microbiome, you can take the Gut Bacteria Balance Quiz in *The Anti-Anxiety Diet* book or complete the Probiotic Challenge worksheet in the Anti-Anxiety Diet Guide at www.alimillerrd.com/anti-anxiety-diet-guide.

A Serving of Culture a Day[1]

Food source and serving	Strains of probiotic present	Influence of probiotic strains and therapeutic food
Kimchi, ⅛–¼ cup	*Lactococcus lactis,* Bifidobacteria, *Lactobacillus kimchii*	Antimicrobial; antioxidant; anti-inflammatory; digestive support; anticancer activity; makes GABA, serotonin, and acetylcholine
Pickled vegetables and sauerkraut, ⅛–¼ cup	Leuconostoc, *Lactobacillus brevis,* Pediococcus pentosaceus, *Lactobacillus plantarum*	Antimicrobial; antioxidant; anti-inflammatory; digestive support; supports repair of leaky gut; anticancer activity; makes GABA, serotonin, and acetylcholine
Raw cacao nibs, 1–2 tablespoons	*Lactobacillus plantarum, Lactobacillus fermentum*	Antimicrobial; supports repair of leaky gut; anti-inflammatory; immune support; makes GABA, serotonin, and acetylcholine
Kombucha, 6–8 ounces	Saccharomyces, Acetobacter, Gluconobacter, Lactobacillus	Antifungal; pathogen-fighting; anti-inflammatory; antioxidant; anticarcinogenic; makes norepinephrine
Miso, 1–2 teaspoons	*Aspergillus oryzae, Lactobacillus acidophilus*	Anticarcinogenic; digestive support; anti-inflammatory; makes GABA, serotonin, and acetylcholine Note: Beyond probiotics, miso contains tyramine, which can increase release of dopamine, epinephrine, and norepinephrine

---

1 Source: https://www.ncbi.nlm.nih.gov/pmc/articles/PMC6191956 and https://www.ncbi.nlm.nih.gov/pmc/articles/PMC5977097

Food source and serving	Strains of probiotic present	Influence of probiotic strains and therapeutic food
Non-denatured whey, 30 grams (about 4 tablespoons)	*Lactobacillus plantarum, Lactobacillus fermentum*	Antimicrobial; supports repair of leaky gut; anti-inflammatory; immune support; makes GABA, serotonin, and acetylcholine
Yogurt and kefir, 6 ounces	*Streptococcus thermophilus, Lactobacillus plantarum,* Bifidobacteria, Saccharomyces	Antimicrobial; antioxidant; anti-inflammatory; digestive support; supports repair of leaky gut; anticancer activity; makes GABA, serotonin, and acetylcholine

Exact colonization of bacteria will vary based on fermentation methods, starter, temperature, and environment, but the noted strains will very likely be present. In addition to a daily probiotic food source, consuming a quality probiotic supplement boosts mood further!

Recipes to Reset Gut Microbiome

❖ *Coconut Cacao Chia Seed Pudding, page 49*

❖ *Steak and Eggs with Chimichurri, page 43*

❖ *Creamy Green Chili Chicken Soup, page 65*

❖ *Kimchi Burger, page 82*

❖ *Cinnamon Protein Nut Butter Balls, page 108*

3. Repair GI Lining

The gut includes both the small and large intestine, which are essential for nutrient absorption and production, housing the immune system and microbiome, detoxification and hydration, neurotransmitter production, and interaction with the central nervous system. If the gut is in an optimal state of health, the lining will be intact, able to prevent large particles or irritants from entering the bloodstream, provide space for good bacteria to thrive, and enhance nutrient absorption.

When the gut is in a stressed state with leaky gut or damage to the delicate internal lining, you are at risk for nutrient deficiency and increased food and chemical sensitivity, as the damaged barrier allows large compounds into the bloodstream, creating an overactive inflammatory response. In addition, when the gut lining is damaged, many of the large particles that enter the bloodstream are more disruptive to brain and mental health as they now may cross the blood-brain barrier and interfere with neurotransmitters.

What Does This Mean for You?

Now that the primary dietary irritants are removed, work toward removing other lifestyle irritants and take proactive measures to reduce or replace them with less toxic options.

Focus on healing your gut lining by adding therapeutic foods to support absorption of nutrients and reduce inflammatory reactions.

Lifestyle Factors for Leaky Gut

Lifestyle irritants include prescription and over-the-counter drugs (including commonly used NSAIDs, antibiotics, and birth control), infections and pathogenic bacteria, chemicals in our tap water, agricultural pesticides, and processed foods, as well as volatile chemicals in cosmetics, fragrances, and households. And, remember, stress itself is a driver. Don't let lifestyle changes overwhelm you. Choose one to two action points to start with from a realistic list of options, such as:

1. Install an in-home reverse osmosis water filtration system.
2. Replace plastic food storage with glass or stainless steel.
3. Stop daily or frequent use of nonsteroidal anti-inflammatory drugs (NSAIDs) and replace them with a natural alternative such as Naturally Nourished Super Turmeric or Inflammazyme formulas.
4. Use basal body temperature (BTT) as natural birth control and wean off the pill.
5. Swap out cosmetics and perfumes with a natural, nontoxic line and essential oils.

Incorporate Therapeutic Foods

Choose from these therapeutic foods to "seal the tank" of your GI tract daily:

Bone Broth: Sip on your broth in a mug, or use it as a cooking liquid, the base of a soup, or even an elixir. Check out Bone Broth 5 Ways on page 14 for tips.

Gelatin: This is a great summer option when bone broth becomes less appealing. Kids love it as gummies or fruited Jell-O. I also add gelatin to many puddings or panna cotta desserts and use it as a thickener in stir-fries and sauces.

Collagen: Perhaps the most versatile of these options, collagen has the least flavor and least influence on texture. Collagen can be used in hot or cold beverages and can be added to any liquid with a quick stir. It is so easy to use I often travel with single packs on the go to boost an unsweetened iced green tea matcha or cold brew.

Bone Broth 5 Ways

To make the recipes below, start with 3 cups of simmering chicken or beef bone broth and add the suggested ingredients with salt and pepper to taste. Makes two (1½-cup) servings.

Base	Add	Directions
Simple Cream of Spinach	• ½ cup onion, sautéed • 3 cups chopped and sautéed spinach • ½ cup full-fat coconut milk	Blend all ingredients on high for 2 minutes until creamy.
Bone Broth Bloody Mary	• 2 cloves garlic, crushed • 2 ounces pickle juice (choose one with live probiotics) • 16 ounces organic tomato juice	Cool broth down to room temperature, then shake with tomato juice to combine. Shake with remaining ingredients on ice, and add hot sauce, to taste.
Turmeric Lime Broth	• Juice of ½ lime • 1 tablespoon dried turmeric • 3 tablespoons coconut oil	Blend all ingredients on high for about 2 minutes until creamy. Top with coarse salt and cilantro.
Umami Mushroom	• ⅔ cup mushrooms, sautéed in sesame oil • 1 tablespoon No-Soy or coconut aminos • Hot sesame oil, to taste	Stir ingredients into broth until well combined, then top with chopped scallions and sesame seeds.
Pesto Perfection	• ½ cup sautéed onion • 1½ cups stewed or sautéed fresh tomatoes • 3 tablespoons pesto	Blend broth on high with the onions and tomatoes for about 2 minutes until creamy, then top with pesto.

Recipes to Repair Your GI Lining

❖ *Avocado Pudding, page 50*

❖ *Crispy Rosemary Chicken with Roasted Brussels Sprouts and Leeks, page 88*

❖ *Anti-Anxiety Diet Bone Broth, page 70*

❖ *Elderberry Gummies, page 142*

❖ *Raspberry Cream Panna Cotta, page 111*

4. Restore Micronutrient Status

Nutritional status directly influences every function of the body. Perpetuated stress response is one reason for micronutrient deficiency. When you are in a chronic state of anxiety or worry, the body burns through antioxidants and B vitamins, as well as specific minerals and amino acids such as magnesium, zinc, selenium, serine, and glutamine. These same nutrients provide the primary compounds that are integral in mood regularity, management of the stress response, and greater resilience. For this reason, they can be a game changer as supplements. This intervention can temper drivers of anxiety by supplementing demand, thus preventing deficiency and symptoms.

A diet that is focused around whole foods with plants in a spectrum of colors and animal products from wild and pasture-raised sources will not only reduce free radicals and inflammation to the brain, it will also drive optimal neurological function and mood stability.

What Does This Mean for You?

It is essential to consume a variety of whole, in-season foods in their most natural form for nutrient density.

Using the recipes in this cookbook, you will combine single-ingredient whole foods, benefit from a synergy of complementary flavors, and eat to absorb the bioavailable nutrients in foods.

To restore micronutrient status, focus on two to three choices from these nutrients:

- **Activated B vitamins:** vitamin B6 (pyridoxine), vitamin B9 (folate), vitamin B12, and inositol

- **Mood-stabilizing minerals:** magnesium, chromium, calcium, and zinc

- **Antioxidants:** selenium, vitamin C, glutathione, and vitamin E

Nutrients to Restore Micronutrient Status

B6 Pyridoxine	**Function:** Cofactor for production of serotonin and GABA; hemoglobin formation; creation of antibodies, methylation support; aids in the production of glutathione; contributes to enhanced antioxidant status **Deficiency symptoms:** Anxiety, depression, ADHD, high blood pressure, rashes and dermatitis, hypothyroidism, fatigue, anemia, muscle pain, tingling hands and feet, seizures, sore glossy tongue, cracked lips **Food sources:** Turkey, pork, halibut, chicken, beef, tuna, salmon, nuts/seeds, bananas, pistachios, carrots, spinach
B9 Folate	**Function:** Cofactor for production of serotonin, dopamine, and epinephrine; supports neuroplasticity; promotes DNA synthesis; aids in amino acid metabolism; produces myelin; supports function of red blood cells and vessel dilation; reduction of homocysteine an inflammatory marker into S-adenosyl-L-methionine (SAMe), a methylation driver of feel-good brain chemicals **Deficiency symptoms:** Anxiety, depression, cognitive decline, insomnia, heart disease, constipation, neuropathy, chronic fatigue, anemia, IBS, poor immune function, restless legs syndrome, birth defects **Food sources:** Spinach, beef liver, asparagus, Brussels sprouts, black-eyed peas, broccoli, avocado *Note: Supplementation with folic acid can drive inflammation and imbalance in neurotransmitters; ensure it is methylfolate or folinic acid.*

B12	**Function:** Cofactor for production of serotonin, GABA, dopamine, and norepinephrine; DNA and RNA synthesis; production of SAMe for methylation support; red blood cell formation; raises cysteine and glutathione levels; aids in nerve function and nerve impulses **Deficiency symptoms:** Anxiety, depression, brain fog, poor circulation, body temperature dysregulation, headaches, insomnia, infertility, muscle weakness, fatigue, shortness of breath, numbness and tingling, swollen tongue, mouth ulcers, constipation **Food sources:** Organ meat, sardines, clams, oysters, mussels, salmon, shellfish, tuna, octopus, beef, lobster, egg yolk, turkey, all animal products
Inositol	**Function:** Favorably modulates serotonin and dopamine receptors; promotes fat utilization; increases levels of adiponectin; female cycle and ovulation regulation; improves insulin receptivity; improves lipid distribution and blood sugar control **Deficiency symptoms:** Anxiety, depression, insomnia, panic attacks, weight gain/ fat deposits, infertility, hormone imbalance, insulin resistance, gestational diabetes, high cholesterol, elevated blood pressure, PCOS, excessive testosterone **Food sources:** Citrus fruit, nuts, seeds, cantaloupe, navy and lima beans *Note: Supplementation is often required to get therapeutic effects; inositol is safe with both children and pregnant women at dosage in 1 scoop of Naturally Nourished Relax and Regulate.*
Magnesium	**Function:** The ultimate chill pill, suppresses excess cortisol; regulates HPA axis; aids in neuromuscular relaxation; involved in over 300 enzyme functions, including activation, neuromuscular activity, membrane transport, and energy metabolism; contributes to calcium and phosphorus metabolism **Deficiency symptoms:** Anxiety, depression, numbness, tingling, seizures, heart palpitations or arrhythmias, nausea, changes in appetite, muscle cramps, chronic fatigue, insomnia, restless legs syndrome, constipation, asthma, high blood pressure, bone loss **Food sources:** Dark leafy greens, almonds, cacao, dark chocolate, Brazil nuts, pumpkin seeds, flax seeds, cashews, halibut, salmon, avocado
Chromium	**Function:** Aids in insulin function and utilization, which allows tryptophan to cross the blood-brain barrier and boost serotonin levels; increases fertility, carbohydrate, and fat metabolism; essential for fetal growth and development **Deficiency symptoms:** Anxiety, depression, fatigue, low stress tolerance, lightheadedness, poor glucose management, metabolic syndrome, unfavorable lipid shifts with elevated LDL and triglycerides, low HDL, weight gain **Food sources:** Broccoli, turkey, green beans, Ceylon cinnamon (cassia cinnamon is okay but has fewer nutrients and antioxidants), beef, red wine, turkey, garlic, prunes, apples

Calcium	**Function:** Regulates neurological function and deficiency; extreme deficiency has been tied to mania, with more moderate levels driving panic, confusion, and chronic anxiety; works inversely with magnesium as an activator versus relaxer in muscles; component of hard tissue; transmission of hormonal information; role in blood clotting, cell membrane function, and muscle tone and contraction
	Deficiency symptoms: Anxiety, depression, confusion, delirium, muscular irritability, muscle spasms, bone loss disorders, tooth decay, periodontal disease, weak and brittle nails, hypertension
	Food sources: Grass-fed dairy products if tolerable (yogurt and quality, casein-free whey are great sources), canned salmon and sardines with bones, leafy greens, chia seed, almonds
	Note: Use of selective serotonin reuptake inhibitor (SSRI) drugs, or antidepressants, increases risk for calcium deficiency and may require supplementation with microcrystalline hydroxyapatite compound (MCHC) form such as Naturally Nourished OsteoFactors
Zinc	**Function:** Aids in optimized stomach acid to break down glutamine to GABA; interacts with NMDA receptors that regulate sleep and neurotransmitters; activates almost 200 enzymes with roles in cell regulation, lipid metabolism, and digestion; component of thymic hormones (immune function) and gustin (taste acuity); maintains integrity of intestinal tract; competes with copper, preventing panic
	Deficiency symptoms: Anxiety, depression, loss of smell/taste, poor immune function, frequent illness, elevated cholesterol, high blood pressure, insulin resistance, hypothyroid, infertility, insomnia, alopecia, acne, weak nails
	Food sources: Oysters, liver (from pasture-raised sources), grass-fed beef and lamb, egg yolk, fish, pork, turkey, molasses, pumpkin seeds, sesame seeds, dark chocolate, nuts
Selenium	**Function:** Both a mineral and an antioxidant, aids in protecting cells from oxidative damage and inflammation; component of the master antioxidant glutathione; recycles vitamins C and E; stimulation of lymphocytes (white blood cells that regulate immune system); converts thyroid hormone T4 into active T3
	Deficiency symptoms: Anxiety, depression, fatigue, weight gain, low red blood cells, arthritis, eczema, psoriasis, impaired immune function, poor glucose management, sore muscles, poor digestion, hypothyroidism
	Food sources: Brazil nuts, mushrooms, tuna, oysters, sardines, shrimp, seafood, liver, cashews, sunflower seeds, garlic, pork, beef, poultry
Vitamin C	**Function:** Used to produce epinephrine and regulate cortisol metabolism and production; most available antioxidant to donate electrons to scavenging, harmful free radicals; inhibits activation of mast cells to regulate histamine levels; plays a role in collagen formation, supporting skin, tendons, ligaments, and vessels
	Deficiency symptoms: Anxiety, depression, irritability, tooth decay, muscle cramps, sore joints, impaired immune function, delayed wound healing, dry skin, bruising, iron deficiency anemia, low platelets, bumpy skin (keratosis pilaris), bright red hair follicles (perifollicular hemorrhage)
	Food sources: Citrus fruit and zest, berries, sweet bell peppers, herbs, cabbage, leafy greens, papaya, guava, mango, tomatoes, rosehips

Glutathione	**Function:** The most preeminent antioxidant in the body made by every cell, regulates the production of proinflammatory cytokines; aiding in enhanced brain function and mood stability; supports cell membrane integrity; repairs damage to cells caused by inflammation; supports the liver and gallbladder **Deficiency symptoms:** Anxiety, depression, chronic fatigue, rapid aging, muscle fatigue, memory problems, macular degeneration, arthritis, impaired immune function, calcification, free radical overload, risk for tumorigenic activity **Food sources:** Cumin, asparagus, broccoli, cauliflower, Brussels sprouts, grass-fed whey protein, arugula, kale, avocado, egg yolk, turmeric
Vitamin E	**Function:** Essential to the central nervous system, protects neurons and cell membranes from oxidative damage; supports neurotransmitter levels otherwise reduced by free radicals, aids in red blood cell formation, aids in utilization of vitamin K, promotes widening of vessels to prevent plaque or clot formation **Deficiency symptoms:** Anxiety, depression, memory issues, weakness, coordination issues, involuntary eye movements, dermatitis, poor skin/hair integrity, psoriasis, anemia, susceptibility to bruising **Food sources:** Almonds, sunflower seeds, hazelnuts, walnuts, Brazil nuts, pine nuts, cashews, pistachios, trout, octopus, avocado, red bell pepper, dark leafy greens, rosemary

Key: Activated B vitamins   Mood-stabilizing minerals   Antioxidants

Recipes to Restore Micronutrient Status

❖ *Savory Pork Hash with Sage Brussels, page 44*

❖ *Sardine Caesar Salad, page 56, with pork rind crumble as crouton*

❖ *Cream of Kale Soup with Crispy Prosciutto Chips, page 61*

❖ *Simple Sneaky Bolognese with Greens, page 86*

❖ *Lemon Lavender CBD Balls, page 112*

5. Rebound Adrenals

The HPA axis is integral to the sympathetic fight-or-flight and the parasympathetic rest-and-digest modes. When the body is in reactive sympathetic mode, the HPA axis focuses toward adrenal stimulation, initially with the output of adrenaline (epinephrine) as a neurotransmitter that drives excitatory response in the body, increasing heart rate, blood pressure, blood sugar, and alertness, followed by a release of cortisol.

When reacting to a predator or shifting to survival mode, the body's stress response is necessary and returns, once safe, to a parasympathetic regulatory state. However, when the HPA axis is activated in modern society, often it is due to a mental, emotional, or physiological stressor that is chronic rather than transient.

Chronic stimulation nullifies the feedback loop and causes a constant leak of cortisol, leading to imbalance in other adrenal compounds, including dopamine, the bliss neurotransmitter; norepinephrine, the balancer for epinephrine, a primary chemical in stress and anxiety expression; DHEA, a steroid hormone that impacts stress resilience and hormone health; and even aldosterone, a hormone that regulates sodium and blood pressure. Each of these compounds has a vital role in your body. It is important to reduce excessive output and rebound fatigued adrenals to benefit from their feel-good influence and anti-inflammatory effects.

Stressed and Wired vs. Stressed and Tired

Both excessive adrenal output and adrenal fatigue can drive anxiety. Beyond a state of mental distress, one may experience increased body fat, insomnia, irritability, tension, and autoimmune disease in an overdrive state, while adrenal fatigue can cause low energy, brain fog, difficulty concentrating, increased histamine response, and a flat affect or depression. When the body is chronically stressed it hinders its parasympathetic state. So there is often imbalance in sleep and energy regulation, digestion, thyroid function, and sexual hormone balance, often driving irregular cycles or infertility as the body doesn't feel "safe" to sleep, burn body fat, or carry a child.

What Does This Mean for You?

Spend some time considering if you are in HPA axis overdrive. Are you "stressed and wired" or in burned-out, "stressed and tired" mode? To assist in this process, use the Adrenal Fatigue and HPA Axis Imbalance quiz in *The Anti-Anxiety Diet*.

Work to reduce the influence of chronic stress by practicing yoga, meditation, grounding or earthing outside (making contact with the earth's electrons), breathwork, and quality restful sleep.

Incorporate adaptogenic herbs, which aid in stress resilience and tolerance, as well as nervines to support relaxation and nervous system protection in your teas, daily morning beverages, and as a supplement to support HPA axis responsiveness.

Consume a diet dominant in fat to support hormone production and adrenal function. Choose from avocado, nuts, seeds, coconut (in all forms), tallow, lard, and fatty cuts of pasture-raised meats and wild-caught fish.

Aim to consume vitamin C–rich foods daily. Vitamin C can be found in the highest concentration in your tiny adrenal glands, where cortisol metabolism, regulation, and production take place. Add berries, bell peppers, citrus zest, and leafy greens to your daily diet to support optimal levels.

Adapta-What?

Adaptogens are a group of traditional herbs that help us to be more resilient to stress, improving our ability to handle stress demands without getting overwhelmed or fatigued. These herbs are very tonifying to the body and optimize thyroid health and metabolic activity. Rather than targeting one pathway, adaptogens are multifocal, hitting many physiological influences in the body to support immune function, focus, and sustained energy. By definition, in order for an herb to be classified as an adaptogen, it must be nontoxic to the recipient, yield support for homeostasis throughout the body, and regulate cortisol.

Adaptogens used in Naturally Nourished supplement formulas and this cookbook include ashwagandha, rhodiola, panax ginseng, cordyceps, and maca.

Recipes to Rebound Adrenals

- ❖ *Citrus Pumpkin Pancakes, page 46*
- ❖ *Broiled Lobster with Avocado Hollandaise, page 91*
- ❖ *Zesty Creamy Carrot Soup, page 63*
- ❖ *Summer Salad with Pickled Onion, page 52*
- ❖ *Keto Citrus Burst Smoothie, page 129*

6. Rebalance Neurotransmitters

The central nervous system releases billions of neurotransmitters, all of which function as biological signals orchestrating a symphony in the brain. They regulate mood, perception, cognitive processing, and many daily functions. Protein compounds called amino acids are the building blocks of neurotransmitters. They combine in the presence of specific enzymes and cofactor nutrients.

Neurotransmitters also play a key role in managing inflammation and cognition and driving many autonomic nervous system functions. To complicate matters, the neurotransmitters of the central nervous system communicate directly with those produced in the gut via the enteric nervous system, which has more neurons than the central nervous system, including the brain and spine, combined.

Neurotransmitters are categorized as either excitatory, stimulating neuron firing, or inhibitory, reducing neuron activity. The stress-responding excitatory neurotransmitters made by the adrenal glands are known as catecholamines. These include dopamine, norepinephrine, and epinephrine to respond in fight-or-flight mode.

Beyond serotonin, GABA is an inhibitory neurotransmitter known for regulating anxiety and depression. GABA is a major chill pill of the brain, inhibiting anxiety and reducing physiological response to stress. Beyond balancing mood and mellowing out the mind, GABA can have anti-inflammatory effects on the gut itself, thus reducing the response of inflammatory chemicals and compounds. It can lower epinephrine, which in excess can drive panic, worry, irritability, and distress.

What Does This Mean for You?

A diet rich in amino acids tryptophan, tyrosine, and glycine will increase GABA production and have a calming effect. This includes clean sources of pasture-raised poultry and pork, grass-fed beef, as well as bone broth, gelatin, and pork skins.

Ensure you are consuming ample protein to provide foundational amino acid support! Wild-caught fish or grass-fed, pasture-raised meats provide a higher-quality source of nutrients without taxing the body with high amounts of proinflammatory compounds found in conventional sources.

How to optimize your neurotransmitter levels:

- Eat enough protein. Aim for ½ gram of protein per pound of body weight as a daily minimum.

- Support utilization and absorption of protein with digestive enzyme support, such as Naturally Nourished Digestaid.

- Get 7 to 9 hours of sleep at night.

- Practice deep breathing.

- Adjust environment to reduce stress and learn to say "no."

- Practice perspective and gratitude.

- Reduce screen time and wear blue blockers, or special lenses that block blue light. Electronics and blue light burn out your dopamine.

- Consider amino acid supplementation such as tryptophan, tyrosine, L-theanine, and serine.

Recipes to Rebalance Neurotransmitters

❖ *Matcha Lime Pudding with Blackberries, page 39*

❖ *Low-Carb Collagen Zucchini Muffins, page 48*

❖ *Turkey Macadamia Nuggets with Liver, page 97*

❖ *Macadamia Coconut–Crusted Halibut, page 90*

❖ *Matcha Blueberry Green Smoothie, page 128*

Chapter 2

The Anti-Anxiety Diet Ketogenic Approach

The anti-anxiety diet starts with a six-week high-fat, low-carb (HFLC) ketogenic approach that allows the body to starve off bacteria overgrowth, support gut restoration if treating leaky gut, quickly reduce common food sensitivities, improve insulin signaling, and promote hormonal balance. The optional transition to a low-glycemic approach offers a more varied and potentially more sustainable diet you can maintain or use to cycle with your HFLC keto plan.

During your program, you will reconnect with your body and have an opportunity to redefine your relationship with food, determining what foods work best for your body and what phase of carbohydrate restriction yields the best outcomes. This program emphasizes whole food ingredients to reset your palate. A big win is that you can learn to crave and feel satiated by nourishing, real food. You can fall in love with the natural sweetness of sun-ripened peach just picked off the branch. You can free yourself from the ever-consuming thoughts of body image, overconsumption, and over-restriction! Not only will the program successfully promote a reset of your system, it will likely support favorable body composition change while leaving you feeling energized, balanced, and grounded.

Why Keto?

Ketones are a form of energy for the body made from fat, both the excess stores in the body as well as that consumed in the diet, that serves as a cleaner, more constant, high-octane fuel source. When not in ketosis and solely running on glucose or blood sugar, which fluctuates greatly, mood and energy shifts can be irregular with glucose elevating with depression and anxiety. The state of nutritional ketosis is natural, safe, and essential for survival as the human body is designed to be a hybrid machine running on both ketones and glucose for optimal health. It is important to understand that when in a state of ketosis, glucose levels are produced but at a lower, more regulated level. When the body makes ketones in the absence of food (during fasting) or in a state of carbohydrate restriction, they provide favorable mechanisms for stabilized energy, satiety or appetite regulation, reduced inflammation, less oxidative stress, and enhanced GABA production to directly reduce anxiety.

Ketones cross the blood-brain barrier, directly fueling the brain while reducing stress response feedback to the fight-or-flight HPA axis of the body. The ketogenic diet regulates a consistent low glucose level, which reduces insulin response to reduce inflammation, while ketones also reduce excitatory neurotransmitters to stabilize your mind and mood.

Benefits of Ketosis on Brain and Mood

- Satiety and hormonal balance with leptin increase

- Enhances GABA

- Increases neurogenesis, or the production of new neurons

- Increases brain-derived neurotrophic factor (BDNF), which aids in survival, growth, and development of neurons for enhanced brain function

- Reduces oxidative stress in the brain

However, in our culture of overconsuming carbohydrates and eating too much too often, most people don't get to experience the benefit of being fat-fueled or running on ketones. Instead they are suffering from the effects of irregular elevated blood sugar. Unlike *The Anti-Anxiety Diet* recipes, which include those that are keto-friendly as well as those that can be used in carb cycling (see page 29) or a low-glycemic approach, all the recipes in this book are keto-friendly. Because all servings fit within the max of 23 grams of carbohydrates, the recipes in this book can all fit within even the most strict guidelines in Phase 1 (see page 25) depending on other complementary meals that day.

Often, malnourishment at both underweight or overweight status is due to a state of gut distress along with consumption of proinflammatory foods that lack nutrient density. When consuming ingredients featured in this book's recipes, you may also benefit from hormone balance from abundant healthy anti-inflammatory fats, which serve as an essential building block for hormone production.

Reduce Cravings with Leptin

When entering into a state of nutritional ketosis, the body increases its production of leptin, a hormone that reduces excitatory stress in the brain to prevent seizure activity and reduce anxiety, as well as quell hunger with satiety. Made in the fat cells of the body and in the small intestine in response to fats in the diet, leptin docks primarily in the hypothalamus, where it directly influences the HPA axis. The anti-anxiety diet stimulates pathways of leptin production both from body fat burn and dietary fat intake.

Benefits of Leptin

- Promotes satiety

- Regulates weight

- Regulates reproductive health and sexual hormone production

- Supports production of thyroid hormone

- Inhibits stress response and cortisol release

Generally speaking, leptin and insulin work hand in hand. A body with high levels of fat in the state of insulin resistance also commonly has leptin resistance, where it doesn't experience satiety signals, leading to chronic overeating and weight gain. Practicing a ketogenic diet will drop insulin levels, which provides access to body fat metabolism and will aid in leptin sensitivity or enhanced signaling.

Typically, calorie restriction and a drop in insulin will drive a drop in leptin, which then signals the body to hunger; however, the ketogenic diet is unique in its ability to lower insulin while increasing leptin levels in the brain. This is likely due to the anti-inflammatory state and high fat intake stimulating production in small intestines.

How to Achieve Nutritional Ketosis

Transitioning into nutritional ketosis requires a diet that restricts carbohydrates, is dominant in fat, and is moderate in protein. To experience ketosis, stick to Phase 1 guidelines, reducing total carbohydrate intake to 30 grams per day via residual carbs in your non-starchy vegetables and healthy fats (see page 25 for Phase 1 guidelines). For example, half of an avocado has 6 to 8 grams of carbs, so, as you can see, 30 grams can add up quickly.

To stick within the 30-gram limitations, in Phase 1 you will be eliminating all starchy vegetables, legumes, and fruits. After a couple days of this restriction, your body will be forced to manufacture ketones as an alternative energy source to glucose. During this transition into ketosis, it is important to ensure electrolyte support and optimal hydration to keep blood pressure stable as fluid levels and stress hormone levels change within your body.

Keto-Flu Prevention Plan

Follow these four essentials and you can avoid the symptoms of keto-flu (aches, palpitations, dizziness, sleep issues, headaches). I also recommend holding off on intermittent fasting when starting the anti-anxiety diet to allow your body to adjust to blood sugar and hormonal shifts (see Second-Guess the Intermittent Fast on page 32).

1. Consume at least half your body weight in fluid ounces of water daily (if you weigh 150 pounds, drink at least 75 fluid ounces).

2. Consume at least (yes, at least) 2 teaspoons daily of a quality sea salt with 60+ trace minerals, such as Redmond Real Salt.

3. Incorporate potassium-rich foods daily, such as avocado, spinach, or coconut water (watch for added sugar in coconut water).

4. Use a quality magnesium bisglycinate supplement at 200 to 500 milligrams, such as Naturally Nourished Relax and Regulate, which also provides the added benefit of inositol for reduction of anxiety and hormone regulation.

Phase 1: Ketogenic Protocol

In ketosis, carbohydrate choices come from residual carbs in non-starchy vegetables, avocados, nuts, and seeds. Reduce total carbohydrate intake to 30 grams per day max. This means no fruit or starchy vegetables; be mindful of avoiding carbohydrate-containing foods.

Follow for weeks 1 through 6 at minimum! You may follow for weeks 1 through 12+ and maintain as a lifestyle.

Macronutrient % distribution:

- 0 to 10% carbs

- 15 to 25% protein

- 65 to 75% fat

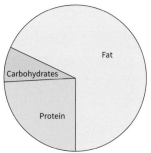

Note: If you are not looking to lose weight, it is possible to maintain a healthy weight and even gain weight if needed while implementing the ketogenic diet.

Most overweight teens who have any of these conditions can thrive in Phase 1 keto: epilepsy, cancer, type 1 diabetes, glycogen storage disease, GLUT1 deficiency disease.

What Is Ketosis?

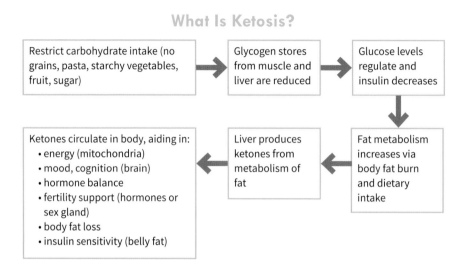

| Restrict carbohydrate intake (no grains, pasta, starchy vegetables, fruit, sugar) | → | Glycogen stores from muscle and liver are reduced | → | Glucose levels regulate and insulin decreases |

Ketones circulate in body, aiding in:
• energy (mitochondria)
• mood, cognition (brain)
• hormone balance
• fertility support (hormones or sex gland)
• body fat loss
• insulin sensitivity (belly fat)
← Liver produces ketones from metabolism of fat ← Fat metabolism increases via body fat burn and dietary intake

Easing Your Transition

Prior to starting Phase 1, kick things off with two weeks without the five inflammatory foods: gluten, corn, soy, dairy, and sugar. This will support the body and brain by reducing inflammation and regulating blood sugar. After two weeks of making this shift, your body will be better able to handle the stricter ketogenic protocol. If you are already coming from a paleo or grain-free, clean whole foods diet or already practicing keto, you may decide to jump right into Phase 1.

Phase 1.5: A Gentle, Low-Carb Approach

Phase 1.5 serves as an optional gentle entry point for an individual who finds the tight nutritional ketosis of Phase 1 too restrictive, such as a pregnant woman, a young child, or a teen entering puberty. Phase 1.5 may also be a sustainable maintenance mode for you once you've shifted your metabolism to be fat-adapted following adherence to the Phase 1 protocol.

What Is Metabolic Flexibility?

After about six weeks of following the Phase 1 guidelines you may choose to bring in berries and liberalize your vegetable intake while still staying well in nutritional ketosis. By now, your body knows the magic of ketones and has the ability to burn fat as fuel. This is metabolic flexibility, the threshold at which your body is able to continue to produce and benefit from ketones while consuming more carbohydrates. Your metabolic flexibility will depend greatly on your muscle mass, stress, exercise, digestive function, and food selection. The freedom of metabolic flexibility allows for a more dynamic diet with a variety of foods, including starchy vegetables and fruits to provide fiber, antioxidants, and unique plant compounds.

Determine Metabolic Flexibility with Phase 1.5

To determine your metabolic flexibility, after six weeks of Phase 1 of the anti-anxiety diet, I encourage advancing to Phase 1.5, which may be the best way to meet the therapeutic food goals of the anti-anxiety diet and maintain a sustainable diet with food freedom while likely still maintaining nutritional ketosis. I personally live between Phase 1 and Phase 1.5, depending on the day and season, and I practice carb cycling to Phase 2 once or twice monthly to support hormone regulation.

Is This Even Keto?

In general, if you want a more even-keeled approach that is less aggressive and supports mood stability without necessarily going ketogenic, you may try starting at Phase 1.5 rather than restricting carbohydrates to less than 30 grams a day as seen in Phase 1.

Phase 1.5 protocol is a more aggressive low-glycemic approach, slightly more carb restricted than Phase 2, and, for some, a sweet spot to maintain benefits of light nutritional ketosis and anti-anxiety effects while maintaining healthy hormonal and metabolic balance. It also may simply serve as a more gentle entry point for those who want the benefits of a low-carb lifestyle when ketosis feels too restrictive or unnecessary. In general, adding carbs may very well kick you out of ketosis, but it may be more favorable for your body based on your unique needs. Remember, the primary goal in the anti-anxiety diet is to heal and balance your body. I am providing you with guidelines on where to start and considerations for selecting your entry point. Ultimately you are as unique as your thumbprint and what works for one person will be very different for another.

Phase 1.5 Protocol

45–75g carbs on average

Macronutrient % distribution:

- 10 to 20% carbs

- 20 to 30% protein

- 55 to 65% fat

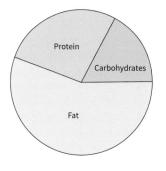

Phase 1.5 is an entry point is for:

- Toddlers, kids at any weight (note they can all fit well in Phase 2 if just supporting growth and development with blood sugar balance and have no neurological, metabolic, or behavioral concerns)

- Children with ADHD, autism, multiple sclerosis, migraines, degenerative or autoimmune disease, traumatic brain injury, and behavioral conditions, depending on the severity of the condition and where therapeutic use of ketones is necessary

- Teens of ideal weight (overweight teens would do great in Phase 1, but if hormones get thrown off, transition them back to Phase 1.5)

- Pregnant women who would benefit from carb control as advised by a medical team (pregnant women with regulated blood sugar levels may start with Phase 2)

- Those with a hypothyroid or autoimmune condition who have previously done poorly with tight carb restriction (this entry may be for to six weeks, then going into Phase 1 is recommended)

How Phase 1.5 Is Different from a Tight Phase 1 Keto

- Less restrictive—if you are stressing about celery, this may be for you.

- No restrictions on non-starchy veggies!

- May include carbs! After liberalizing to 45 grams of carbs with unlimited non-starchy vegetables, you may determine you feel even better with intermittent carb inclusion beyond this level with a daily selection of one choice of fruit or starchy vegetables.

- Carbs to consider in evening meal: beets, berries, green plantain/banana, sweet potato, butternut squash or pumpkin, rainbow carrots, sweet potatoes (for produce inspiration, check out the Grocery List from the Anti-Anxiety Diet Guide at www.alimillerrd.com/anti-anxiety-diet-guide).

Phase 2: Low-Glycemic Protocol

After six weeks of tight ketosis and allowing your body to convert to using fat instead of sugar as its primary fuel, you will have an opportunity to transition or intermittently cycle to the less carb-restrictive Phase 2. Phase 2 is low-glycemic, with a limit of 75 to 120 grams of carbs. It may be appropriate to fully transition to Phase 2 sooner if you are feeling low energy on Phase 1 protocol or if you are having unfavorable symptom shifts (such as worsened mood, sleep disturbances, or undesired weight loss).

In Phase 2, carbs, fruits, and starchy vegetables are permitted to provide dietary variety, beneficial fibers, support of serotonin expression, and a leptin response reset. Phase 2 eating can be seen as an approach to carb cycling while maintaining ketosis the majority of the time. Carb cycling may be done based on times of hormone shifts or randomly on a couple Saturdays a month to create a sustainable approach and more social freedom. Favorable effects such as improved ketone production, hormone balance, and reduced stress response can be seen when cycling carbs after becoming adapted to using fat as your primary fuel. However, if you experienced beneficial mood-stabilizing outcomes from the Phase 1 ketogenic approach, consider holding off on transitioning to Phase 2, or not doing so at all.

Increase total carbohydrate intake to a maximum of 75 to 120 grams per day. This means adding in fruit, starchy vegetables, and carbohydrate-containing foods.

Macronutrient % distribution:

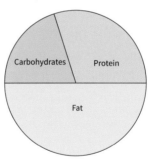

- 20 to 30% carbs

- 25 to 35% protein

- 45 to 55% fat

Carb Cycling 101

Choose two to three carb servings (one carb serving is 15 grams of carbohydrates; examples of a serving include ½ cup sweet potato, 1 small apple, 1 date).

Carb choices should be consumed in the evening to enhance serotonin and melatonin.

Carb cycling resets the hormetic impact of carb restriction and drives insulin release, which stimulates leptin production.

For women who are menstruating, carb cycling should be considered at ovulation and menstruation (typically days 1 to 2 and days 17 to 18 of their 28-day cycle) to support hormonal influences on mood, cravings, and anxiety.

Individuals with hypothyroidism and adrenal fatigue benefit from carb cycling once or twice a month.

People with low body fat tend to benefit from carb cycling, as their leptin levels are generally lower.

If prone to low leptin due to fasting or high stress, it is beneficial to carb cycle one to two times per month. See signs of low leptin below to determine if carb cycling would be beneficial for you.

If you notice a decline in your progress when you transition to Phase 2 or carb cycle, you may consider going back to Phase 1 for four to six weeks prior to trying Phase 2 again, if desired.

Is Carb Cycling Necessary?

Most men and some women are able to stay in Phase 1 carb restriction for extended periods of time and continue to reap the benefits; women, however, due to hormonal demands, may over time get leptin depletion with dynamic drops in leptin levels and may experience sexual hormone dysfunction such as loss of cycle, ovulation, or infertility. This is where the simple strategy of carb cycling can serve to reset the body's metabolic process and keep the body in a regulatory mode with signals ensuring the body it is safe and supporting regulatory and reproductive function.

Carb Restriction and Low Leptin

Since leptin levels are produced by body fat, individuals at lower body fat are more susceptible to dips in leptin during Phase 1. Fats in the diet aid in satiety and some level of leptin production. In addition, leptin intake is required for other mechanisms in the body that may require a boost of insulin via a carb-up to support leptin demands when body fat reserves aren't ample. Cycling nutrient-dense carbs is a simple solution to avoid interference with regulatory body function.

Signs of low leptin:

- Insomnia
- Loss of period or irregular menstrual cycle
- Hormonal imbalance
- Irritability
- Anxiety
- Hypothyroid

When leptin levels drop, the body goes into survival mode and suppresses metabolic function, thyroid output, and sexual hormone production, leading to missed periods, infertility, and anxiety. When leptin levels don't register at the hypothalamus, thyroid-releasing hormone and gonadotropin hormone decrease and cortisol signaling goes up.

- If you suspect low leptin levels, consider carb cycling weekly or monthly. See Carb Cycling 101 on page 29.

- Support your HPA axis with nervines and adaptogens. Get 8 hours of sleep to support leptin levels.

- Even if your appetite gets suppressed, ensure you are getting enough fat to support hormone production.

There is no perfect approach to carb exploration and discovering your metabolic flexibility. You may notice that you feel better in Phase 1 ketosis during certain seasons, levels of stress, variances in exercise, and lifecycle demands, whereas other times maintaining low-glycemic Phase 2 as a daily diet or frequent carb cycling feels appropriate. If you allow the concept of a perfect diet to override connection with your body and its needs, you will likely not heal or get favorable results. Resist getting dogmatic with macronutrients (or macros) once you have experienced fat adaptation. Rather than following inflexible guidelines on numbers and percentages, listen to your body and feed it real food that it performs best on. Focus on the primary tenets of *The Anti-Anxiety Diet* by using the Foundational 6 Rs approach and food-as-medicine support as priorities to yield best outcomes!

Ketosis as a Stressor

For those of you who feel amazing on keto and want to maintain a restricted level of carbohydrate intake, it may be absolutely appropriate, but you must consider that the ketogenic diet is a hormetic stressor that compounds other stressors, such as lack of quality sleep, calorie restriction, increased exercise, recovery from an injury, increased mental demands, and time-restricted eating, also known as intermittent fasting. I call it the type A female trifecta, but really it is like four to five contributors: the mom who is over-caffeinated, under-rested, overworked, and then trying to eat the "perfect" macros for ketosis as well as increase exercise and incorporate intermittent fasting. This situation leads to destruction, often putting the sympathetic fight-or-flight system into overdrive and leaving the woman in a buzzing flurry of imbalance in the brain and body. Now this is not technically keto's fault; however, many people who go keto lose their appetite and increase their energy, so they push both restriction and increased output, increasing stress and adding more health challenges.

When your body is in the state of ketosis, it experiences cellular signal shifts serving as a form of stress that may ultimately yield enhanced metabolic function, just as exercise or the use of a sauna may. With exercise, the body goes through some level of increased oxidative stress, but the stimulant exposure makes it stronger, more resilient, and ultimately able to manage at a lower level of oxidative stress.

Often, individuals on the ketogenic diet lose their appetite. This, paired with the known benefits of fasting, can be appealing. However, this can burn out the HPA axis and create food insecurity signals or distress in the system. If you add too many things at once (including intensive exercise or calorie restriction), the body may respond unfavorably to nutritional ketosis and you may need to transition to Phase 2 of the anti-anxiety diet. Once you are fat-adapted at about six to eight weeks into the first phase of the anti-anxiety diet, intermittent fasting may be appropriate, as the body has adapted to the hormetic shifts of ketosis as well as positive shifts in inflammation and nutrient influx.

Anything, however, can be distressing for the body, hindering parasympathetic function and negatively impacting digestion, energy, hormones, and metabolism. This is where the flexibility and fluidity within the phases of the anti-anxiety diet helps with whole-body balance. Adjust your phase of carbohydrate restriction and time-restricted eating based on other stressors to allow for whole body balance. Rigidity may yield imbalance and ultimately more stress to the system. The benefits of nutritional ketosis far outweigh the risks of low leptin levels, but it is important to ensure when feeling a boost of energy that you don't overcommit or overextend.

Keto Recipes

How are all the recipes in here keto if there are non-keto foods in them?

When starting a ketogenic diet, a list of restricted foods can help with structure. However, to make this diet approach sustainable for the long haul, many people reach for processed sugar-free items like keto bars, ice cream, and other products that use chemical additives, non-caloric sweeteners, and ultimately have more grams of total carbs. Rather than jack up your metabolism and mess with your palate by maintaining an unnatural expectation of sweet, think outside the box to achieve a balanced whole-food approach.

It is important to remember ketosis is a metabolic state, not a food list. When you focus on single-ingredient foods for nourishment while listening to your body's feedback signals, you can really redefine your relationship with food and start to determine which foods serve you best. I choose to use whole, single-ingredient, non-processed ingredients in my recipes. This means you will see mashed banana, dates, raw honey, and robust maple within some of these recipes. Consuming them within a balanced low-carb, fat-fueled day will still yield a state of nutritional ketosis (see the One-Week Sample Meal Plan on page 38 or the Four-Week Meal Plan in the Anti-Anxiety Diet Guide at www.alimillerrd.com/anti-anxiety-diet-guide. Focusing on whole real foods often means nutrient density and less distressful or potentially irritating compounds to your digestion, microbiome, and metabolism.

Why I Don't Do Net Carbs

Net carbs are the grams of carbohydrates remaining after subtracting fiber and sugar alcohols from the total carbohydrate. Many people follow net carbs and will select food products that have a low net carb. The food industry caught on to this and began adding industrial fibers to offset carb ratio. I value fiber intake from whole food sources. I provide the fiber content in all of these recipes so you can see its contribution to your microbiome to support detoxification and metabolic function. Although I value fiber, I use total carbs but don't subtract grams. Fiber in foods will offset the glucose influence, but this varies by individual. I also don't recommend making food decisions based on labeled packages and limit the intake of industrial fibers that may irritate the gut.

Why Whole Foods Matter

My food-as-medicine philosophy is focused on whole real foods that have not been processed, stripped, refined, or chemically treated. With an anti-anxiety diet approach, it is important to support sustainable results by avoiding food-like substances that often include inflammatory, gut-irritating, or microbiome-influencing ingredients. When considering whether your food selection is whole, as yourself:

- Can you imagine it growing?

- Are all of its edible parts intact?

- What has been done to it since harvest?

- Have chemical solvents been added to manufacture or extract it?

Choosing Your Sweeteners

When choosing between a date or raw unfiltered honey versus erythritol or stevia powder, there is a clear separation between whole real food and chemicals. Even if erythritol is derived from non-GMO corn, it is still highly processed. There is zero possibility of you creating it from an ear of corn in your kitchen or house; you'd need some kind of *Breaking Bad* setup in your garage to turn corn into an odorless, perfectly proportioned, white powder.

Regardless of what phase of carb restriction you are on, I strongly suggest avoiding non-caloric sweeteners such as erythritol, xylitol, or other sugar alcohols, as well as plant-derived sweeteners from stevia and monk fruit. Instead, learn to reset your palate to appreciate subtle sweetness from foods that provide nourishment and other health-supporting benefits. All the whole food sweeteners are richer and more complex than sugar so they can often be used in smaller volume while providing quite an impact on the palate.

Why I Hate Non-Caloric Sweeteners

1. They are not a whole real food. The exception to this is a ground green stevia leaf which has limited application and versatility in that form as it is quite bitter; even a stevia leaf in whole form should be avoided for the reasons below.

2. They provide a false flavor profile that is excessively sweet and perpetuates cravings. Consuming non-caloric sweeteners that are hundreds of times sweeter than sugar maintains the standard American sterile palate that can't appreciate the natural sweetness of an almond.

3. They create a psychosomatic response in the body. A sweet taste evokes various physiological responses, signaling that food or calories are arriving in the gut. The sweet taste response to non-caloric sweeteners both on the tongue receptors as well as in the gut drive hormone release or reduced sensitivity to insulin, glucagon-like peptide 1 (GLP-1), and ghrelin (the hunger hormone that opposes leptin effects in the body), driving potential blood sugar drops and imbalance, weight gain, and hunger.

4. They interfere with digestive process and gut microbiome. Chemical non-caloric sweeteners as well as natural forms such as Reb A from stevia leaf, have been shown in research to sterilize the microbiome with bacteriostatic properties, in some cases slashing probiotic activity by 50 percent or greater.

5. They are devoid of nutritional value and may even drive deficiency. Non-caloric sweeteners provide no vitamins, minerals, or antioxidants—they actually may interfere with nutrient absorption and antioxidant activity.

Health Benefits of Real Food Sweeteners

Real food sweetener	Health benefits
Raw unfiltered honey	• Antioxidant-rich polyphenols • Chrysin aids in hormone balance and reducing estrogen dominance • Immune boost with seasonal pollen • Prebiotic function supporting microbiome; antifungal and antibacterial defense • B vitamins, calcium, magnesium, potassium • Works well with bright citrus acids, complexity of flavor varies with region
Dark amber maple syrup	• Antioxidant-rich polyphenols as well as catechin, epicatechin, rutin, and quercetin • Anti-inflammatory and anticancer effects • Zinc, manganese, potassium • Robust flavor profile works with rich flavors to offset balsamic or rustic flavors
Coconut	• Antioxidant-rich polyphenols, flavonoids, and anthocyanidins • Medium chain triglycerides (MCTs) in products containing fat aid in ketone production • Minerals concentrated in coconut water (as well as in milk and flesh) support electrolyte balance • Naturally contains inulin, which serves as a prebiotic to support microbiome; lauric acid and caprylic acid support immune function and fight against yeast and bacteria overgrowth • Rich flavor profile provides more complexity and caramelization; contributes to a drier baked good
Dates	• Antioxidant-rich flavonoids and polyphenols • Binds to oxytocin receptors in brain, aiding in bliss • Magnesium, potassium, manganese, vitamin B6 • Mood-boosting due to anti-inflammatory effects and as a source of B6; required in the synthesis of GABA, dopamine, and serotonin • Ground dried date sugar provides moisture and binding; contributes to a more moist baked good with higher glycemic index than sugar; can use less rather than a 1:1 ratio
Banana	• Antioxidant-rich beta-carotene, lutein, selenium, and vitamins A, C, and E • Provides anti-inflammatory mucus in digestive tract, aiding in repairing ulcerations • Tryptophan-rich food paired with a nice boost of B6 aids in serotonin production • Potassium, B vitamins, and vitamin C • Prebiotic fiber supports microbiome • Mashed can provide moisture, binding, and starchy fill with mild sweetness. Works well in nut flour–based quick breads and muffins.

Real food sweetener	Health benefits
Berries	• Antioxidant-rich polyphenols, flavonoids, anthocyanidins, and vitamin C
	• Neurogenesis and reduced inflammatory process in the brain essential for intelligence and mood regulation
	• Vitamin C, vitamin K, manganese, potassium, and folate
	• Provides fiber to support microbiome and anti-adhesive compounds to prevent UTI and bacteria overgrowth
	• Freeze-dried berries are a great add-in to create a tannic bittersweet bite to nut mixes and indulgences. Frozen or fresh mashed berries provide moisture and volume; may work with quick breads and muffins, great in smoothies and purees.

Applying the Anti-Anxiety Diet

- Eat real foods in their most whole, unprocessed form.

- Aim for organic or local and sustainable whenever possible. Remove the Environmental Working Group's list of the most pesticide-laden items, the Dirty Dozen, from your diet. Go to ewg.org/foodnews for a full list.

- Consume 2 to 3 cups of leafy greens daily. Select from a variety of seasonal produce, ideally in wild or heirloom varieties, such as rainbow chard, mizuna, dandelion greens, lacinato kale, etc. Also, consider sprouts as a nutrient-dense option—⅛ cup is equivalent to 1 cup of greens!

- Prioritize fats as the highest contributor of macros. This goes for Phase 1, 1.5, and 2 of your anti-anxiety diet, with healthy fats driving the caloric distribution and carb control based on phase.

- Consume protein in all meals (aim for ½ gram of protein per pound of body weight as a daily minimum).

- Get four to five colors on your plate throughout the day. This is one way to ensure full-spectrum antioxidant coverage and a variety of vitamins and minerals!

- Have a cultured food at least four times per week. This includes ⅛ cup of cultured vegetables such as kraut, kimchi, or pickles, 4 to 6 ounces of kombucha, and 6 ounces of homemade coconut yogurt. To determine your state of microbiome balance, use the Probiotic Challenge worksheet from the Anti-Anxiety Diet Guide at www.alimillerrd.com/anti-anxiety-diet-guide.

- Aim to have 6 to 8 ounces of bone broth four times per week and gelatin and collagen-rich foods throughout the week. This can be the beverage you sip in the evening, a base for soups or stews, or as a liquid to aid in braising and sautéing.

- Eat in a relaxed state, focused on nourishment with silence, music, or conversation. No screens, working, or driving during meal time. Focus on breath and getting into rest-and-digest mode throughout the day, especially at mealtimes to promote digestive enzyme release, optimize absorption of nutrients, and reduce gastric stress.

- Listen to signs of physical hunger and don't eat if you aren't hungry. "Hara hachi bu" is a Confucian phrase that translates to "eat until only 80 percent full." It is used by the Okinawan people who are said to be the longest lived (many up to or just over the age of 100), healthiest, and happiest people on the planet. Stop before you get full to prevent distress to the digestive tract and mindless overeating.

Each recipe in this cookbook falls within the guidelines of the anti-anxiety diet. All recipes featured are gluten-free, corn-free, soy-free, and sugar-free. Look for tags identifying potential allergens or irritants in the recipes: (nf) **nut-free**   (ef) **egg-free**

Use the one-week sample meal plan on page 38 to apply the structure and guidelines of the anti-anxiety diet. This week-long plan ranges from Phase 1 to Phase 1.5 intake, which can be varied with simple adjustments. To ensure you stay in Phase 1 using this meal plan, consider restricting residual carbs in one of the meals or snacks. You can also potentially skip the suggested snack altogether or swap it out with a carb-free option. These adjustments will be based on your body composition and metabolic flexibility if you are looking to stay in Phase 1 tight nutritional ketosis. If you are looking to maintain or experience a more liberalized fat-fueled approach, consider eating as is and even adding a starchy vegetable or fruit choice. For even more variety, check out the Four-Week Meal Plan from the Anti-Anxiety Diet Guide at www.alimillerrd.com/anti-anxiety-diet-guide.

This plan is developed for 1,400 to 1,600 calories to provide 20 to 35 grams of carbs, 70+ grams of protein, and 90 to 130 grams of fat daily.

This may be too much or too little based on your current weight and body composition goals, movement or exercise, and other metabolic factors. Once you are fat-adapted and feel your anxiety has reduced and blood sugar has stabilized, you could play with doing a fat fast in the morning with 150–200 calories of fat from coconut oil, cacao butter, or MCT oil added to hot tea or the occasional cup of coffee, or consumed as a concentrated fat bite such as the Lemon Lavender CBD Balls on page 112.

One-Week Sample Meal Plan

	Breakfast	Lunch	Snack	Dinner
SUN	1 serving Steak and Eggs with Chimichurri (page 43)	1 serving Almond Butter Berry Smoothie (page 128)	½ oz pork rinds dipped in ½ avocado mashed with sea salt + lime	1 serving Herb-Crusted Pork Tenderloin (page 81) 1 serving Crispy Brussels with Umi Plum Vinegar (page 75)
MON	3 oz chicken sausage link, ¼ cup sautéed onion, ½ cup sautéed kale in 1 tsp coconut oil, served with ¼ cup sauerkraut	1 serving Thai Green Curry Chicken Soup (page 66)	1 serving Chia Cherry Thumbprint Cookies (page 118)	1 serving Greek Meatballs with Fresh Herbs (page 84) 1 serving Roasted Mediterranean Vegetables (page 78)
TUE	1 serving Turmeric Lime Broth (page 14) topped with ½ avocado	1 serving Matcha Blueberry Green Smoothie (page 128)	2 hard-boiled eggs with 1 tsp mustard	1 serving Roasted Red Pepper Bisque (page 68) 4 oz rotisserie chicken
WED	1 serving Coconut Cacao Chia Seed Pudding (page 49)	1 serving Thai Green Curry Chicken Soup (page 66)	1 serving Chia Cherry Thumbprint Cookies (page 118)	1 serving Greek Meatballs with Fresh Herbs (page 84) 1 serving Roasted Mediterranean Vegetables (page 78)
THUR	12 oz matcha tea blended with 1 tbsp coconut oil + 1 scoop collagen 2 tbsp almond butter + ¼ cup berries	1 serving Cacao Coconut Cashew Shake (page 130)	1 serving Anti-Anxiety Diet Bone Broth (page 70)	1 serving Roasted Red Pepper Bisque (page 68) 4 oz rotisserie chicken
FRI	1 serving Coconut Cacao Chia Seed Pudding (page 49)	1 serving Kimchi Burger (page 82)	1 serving Savory Ranch Kale Chips (page 71)	1 serving Sardine Caesar Salad (page 56), with pork rind crumble as crouton 2 soft-boiled eggs
SAT	2 eggs 2 slices bacon ½ avocado sprinkled with sea salt	1 serving Golden Lemon Zinger with Coconut Pistachios and Shrimp (page 60)	1 serving Almond Collagen Hot Cocoa (page 131)	1 serving Garlicky Pesto Shrimp on Spaghetti Squash (page 94)

Chapter 3

Breakfast

Matcha Lime Pudding with Blackberries (nf) (ef)

FOOD AS MEDICINE   Start your day with this creamy, zesty pudding that blends grassy matcha tea powder with the light, bright acidic notes of lime and blackberries. Matcha provides L-theanine, an amino acid compound that supports a mellow alertness and aids in alpha brainwave expression. Eat as a dense snack or a light meal—you can easily bulk up with additional toppings, such as chopped nuts, coconut shreds, or hemp seeds.

Makes: 4 (½ cup) servings | **Prep time:** 5 to 10 minutes | **Set time:** 8 to 10 hours

1 (13.5-ounce) can full-fat coconut milk

2 teaspoons matcha tea powder

1 tablespoon lime zest

2 tablespoons lime juice

½ teaspoon lemon extract or lemon juice

1 tablespoon honey

1 tablespoon gelatin

1 cup fresh blackberries

1. Combine all the ingredients except the blackberries in a blender and mix on high for 1 minute. Let rest for 5 minutes to bloom the gelatin, then blend on high for 1 additional minute.

2. Divide the pudding into 4 ramekins or mason jars and refrigerate for 8 to 10 hours or overnight.

3. Top each ramekin with about ¼ cup blackberries prior to serving.

Nutrition facts per serving

Calories: 232 | Carbohydrates: 12g | Fiber: 3g | Protein: 6g | Fat: 18g

Perfect Egg Cob Salad with Fresh Herbs (nf)

FOOD AS MEDICINE   Salad for breakfast? This recipe is my favorite way to start the day. Lemon and olive oil are fantastic foods to include when breaking your fast as they stimulate bile flow, which in turn stimulates the liver and activates both the detox and digestive processes. Adding bitter radish further supports liver function and provides glucosinolates and indoles, known to enhance detoxification and thus reduce inflammation in the body. Combine the digestive and detox support with a dose of B6 and the choline in the egg yolk and bacon to create a synergy as powerful as it is beautiful!

Makes: 4 servings | **Prep time:** 10 to 15 minutes | **Cook time:** 10 to 12 minutes

8 ounces bacon

1 watermelon radish, thinly sliced into half moons

1 head butter lettuce, cored, with leaves torn into bite-size pieces

¼ cup torn fresh basil, loosely packed

¼ cup torn fresh mint, loosely packed

⅓ cup lemon juice

2 tablespoons white balsamic vinegar

¼ cup olive oil

1 teaspoon mustard

½ teaspoon salt

freshly ground black pepper, to taste

2 small cloves garlic, chopped (about 1 teaspoon)

2 avocados, pitted and sliced

6 soft-boiled eggs, peeled and halved

1. Preheat the oven to 400°F. Place the bacon on a baking sheet and bake for 10 to 12 minutes. Let cool, then tear into 1-inch pieces.

2. Place the radish, lettuce, basil, and mint in a large salad bowl.

3. Combine the lemon juice, white balsamic vinegar, olive oil, mustard, salt, pepper, and garlic in a small jar. Secure the lid and shake for 2 to 3 minutes to emulsify.

4. Toss the greens with the dressing.

5. Top with the avocado slices, soft-boil eggs, and bacon pieces.

Nutrition facts per serving

Calories: 430 | Carbohydrates: 9g | Fiber: 4g | Protein: 21g | Fat: 35g

How to Make Perfect Soft-Boiled Eggs

In a small stock pot, bring 3 to 4 cups of water to a boil, then reduce to a simmer. Gently add the eggs to the pan, cover, and simmer on low heat for 7 minutes. Fill a medium bowl with cold tap water and 2 to 3 ice cubes. At the 7-minute mark, transfer the eggs from the hot pan to the cold water, which rapidly brings down the temperature. Allow to soak in the cold water for about 2 minutes. Peel under cold running water or keep in the shell and store in the fridge for up to 2 days.

Frittata with Greens, Butternut Squash, and Thyme

(nf)

FOOD AS MEDICINE Eggs are bursting with choline, a precursor to acetylcholine (the conductor of brain chemicals). Primarily found in the yolks, choline aids in memory, mood, and brain function. The butternut squash adds a natural sweetness while providing magnesium, potassium, carotenoids, and vitamin C to support relaxation and adrenals; it's also a wonderful source of tryptophan, which builds serotonin. The leafy greens are a rich source of folate.

Makes: 6 slices | Prep time: 15 minutes | Cook time: 55 to 60 minutes

12 eggs

¼ cup full-fat coconut milk

½ teaspoon ground turmeric

1 teaspoon salt, divided

½ teaspoon freshly ground black pepper

2 tablespoons avocado oil, divided

2 cups roughly chopped onion

1 cup butternut squash, cut into ½-inch cubes

4 to 5 collard green leaves, stemmed and chopped (about 3 cups)

5 to 7 thyme sprigs, stemmed and chopped

12 slices cooked bacon, chopped or torn

1. Preheat the oven to 350°F.

2. Whisk the eggs, coconut milk, turmeric, salt, and pepper in a large bowl.

3. Heat a cast-iron skillet or ovenproof pan over medium heat. Add 1 tablespoon of avocado oil, onion, and squash pieces to the pan, stir to coat with oil, and then allow to sit for 15 minutes, stirring every 3 to 4 minutes.

4. Once the onion and squash mixture is softened and caramelized, add the chopped greens and the remaining avocado oil. After about 3 minutes, as the greens start to reduce in size, add the thyme and bacon pieces, and stir the pan one final time.

5. Pour the egg mixture into the pan and do not stir or agitate. Turn the heat down to low heat. When tiny bubbles appear on the surface, about 5 to 6 minutes, transfer the pan to the oven and bake for 20 to 30 minutes, checking at the 20-minute mark. When the frittata has risen about 1 inch and the top layer is cooked through, remove it from the oven and allow it to rest for 4 to 5 minutes before slicing into six pieces.

Nutrition facts per slice

Calories: 280 | Carbohydrates: 10g | Fiber: 3g | Protein: 19g | Fat: 19g

Steak and Eggs with Chimichurri (nf)

FOOD AS MEDICINE The chimichurri's fresh parsley, oregano, and basil have antimicrobial, antibacterial, and antifungal properties and support the removal of bad bacteria. Combined with garlic and olive oil, two other potent fighters, this flavor-packed sauce makes a dip-with-a-kick that resets your microbiome! You can also serve Bacteria-Battling Chimichurri as a spread on roasted lamb, beef, or vegetables such as carrots. This recipe also serves nicely as a dip for raw veggies and can be mixed into scrambled eggs or added on top of an avocado half.

Makes: 2 servings | **Prep time:** 10 to 15 minutes | **Cook time:** 15 minutes

1 (8-ounce) sirloin steak

1 tablespoon avocado oil

4 eggs

salt, to taste

freshly ground black pepper, to taste

Bacteria-Battling Chimichurri (page 136)

1. Heat a large cast-iron or stainless-steel skillet over medium-high heat. When the pan is hot, add the steak and reduce the heat to medium. For a 1-inch-thick sirloin, cook for 5 minutes until the blood starts to seep through, then flip and cook for another 4 to 5 minutes for medium-rare. Remove from the pan and set steak aside to rest while you prepare the eggs.

2. Heat a medium pan over medium heat and add the avocado oil. Once the oil is heated, about 1 minute, crack the eggs into the pan.

Sprinkle with salt and black pepper, and cook for 3 to 4 minutes for sunny-side-up eggs. For eggs over easy, flip at 2 to 3 minutes and cook for an additional 2 minutes on the other side.

3. Slice the steak into strips, divide evenly onto two plates, and drizzle the chimichurri over the meat. Place 2 eggs on the side or on top of the meat, adding more sauce as desired or reserving leftover sauce for another use.

Nutrition facts per serving

Calories: 393 | Carbohydrates: 3g | Fiber: 1g | Protein: 24g | Fat: 31g

Savory Pork Hash with Sage Brussels (nf)

FOOD AS MEDICINE This dish is like Thanksgiving in a bowl. The fresh herbs and crispy pork provide savory flavor while the butternut squash adds a touch of sweetness along with antioxidants and a serotonin boost. (If your carbohydrate tolerance is low, eat less squash.) The fried egg topper marries all the flavors and elevates this dish to OMG status while keeping you grounded, whether you are starting the day or ending it.

Makes: 6 servings | Prep time: 15 minutes | Cook time: 45 minutes

2 tablespoons olive oil

1½ cups diced yellow onion

1 teaspoon salt, divided

1½ cups butternut squash, cut into ½-inch cubes

4 cups thinly sliced Brussels sprouts, trimmed

3 tablespoons chopped fresh sage

2 tablespoons chopped fresh thyme leaves

6 tablespoons chicken bone broth

1 pound ground pork

¼ teaspoon white pepper

1 tablespoon avocado oil

6 eggs

1. Heat a large skillet over medium heat. Add the olive oil and onion, stirring to coat. Once coated, allow the onion to cook undisturbed for 3 to 4 minutes until softened and beginning to brown.

2. Add ¾ teaspoon salt and squash, stir to coat. Once coated, allow to cook undisturbed for 5 minutes.

3. Stir the squash and onion to loosen anything sticking to the pan, then add the Brussels sprouts, sage, and thyme, stirring to coat in the onions and fat.

4. Sauté, stirring every 1 to 2 minutes for another 5 minutes until the veggies begin to stick. Add the broth, 2 tablespoons at a time about every 5 minutes or so, stirring occasionally and cooking for another 15 to 20 minutes over medium-low heat.

5. As the vegetables are cooking, in a separate medium pan over medium heat, cook the pork with the remaining ¼ teaspoon salt and white pepper until slightly pink, about 5 to 6 minutes. Transfer to the vegetable pan.

6. Stir together veggies and pork, and allow to simmer on low for an additional 4 to 5 minutes.

7. While the flavors are combining, in a separate small or medium pan, fry the eggs in avocado oil. Sprinkle with salt and black pepper to taste and cook for 3 to 4 minutes for sunny-side-up eggs or flip at 2 to 3 minutes and cook for 2 minutes more for eggs over easy.

8. Divide hash into six servings (about 1 cup each) and top each with a fried egg.

Nutrition facts per serving

Calories: 346 | Carbohydrates: 17g | Fiber: 5g | Protein: 18g | Fat: 23g

Citrus Pumpkin Pancakes

FOOD AS MEDICINE   Although technically a starchy vegetable, pumpkin is a keto-friendly way to deliver mood-stabilizing amino acids as well as the electrolytes potassium and magnesium. This recipe provides a rich source of antioxidants, including vitamin E and vitamin A, all while balancing out the carbs with soluble fiber and blunting the blood sugar impact from the fats found in nut butters and almond flour. Pairing pumpkin with an additional antioxidant boost of orange zest gives a light, bright flavor and emulates sweet without the addition of maple syrup.

Makes: 4 (2-pancake) servings | Prep time: 10 minutes | Cook time: 5 minutes

½ cup cooked pumpkin

4 eggs

1 teaspoon vanilla extract

2 orange segments

4 teaspoons orange zest, divided
(from about 1 large orange)

3 tablespoons cashew butter

1 tablespoon coconut butter

1½ tablespoons collagen peptides

⅛ cup almond flour

½ teaspoon ground cinnamon

¼ teaspoon ground ginger

¼ teaspoon baking soda

4 to 6 teaspoons avocado oil, divided

4 tablespoons coconut cream

1. In a blender, combine everything but the avocado oil and coconut cream, and blend on high for 45 seconds.

2. Heat a 10- to 12-inch cast-iron skillet or stainless-steel pan and add 2 teaspoons of avocado oil to the pan. Allow it to heat rapidly for 30 to 45 seconds, then reduce the heat to medium.

3. Slowly pour the batter into the pan to make 3 to 4 pancakes, about ⅛ cup batter per pancake. Once tiny bubbles start to form, 1½ to 2 minutes, flip the pancakes and cook for 1½ to 2 minutes more. Remove from the pan and continue until all the batter is gone, adding avocado oil to the pan at the start of each new batch. You may have 2 to 3 batches depending on the size of the pancakes and the pan.

4. As the pancakes are cooking, mix together the coconut cream and remaining 2 teaspoons orange zest in a small bowl. Dollop on pancakes when ready to serve.

Nutrition facts per serving

Calories: 315 | Carbohydrates: 12g | Fiber: 5g | Protein: 11g | Fat: 25g

Low-Carb Collagen Zucchini Muffins

FOOD AS MEDICINE   Thanks to the high-fat almond flour, this zucchini muffin is 70 percent fat macros. Six eggs and collagen peptides (along with the nut flour) pack in the protein as well as gut and connective tissue support. A whole cup of shredded zucchini with skin on provides lutein, zeaxanthin, and beta-carotene, along with minerals and fiber. Adding just a tablespoon of coconut flour creates a perfect mouthfeel and texture. Now here is the kicker: The mashed banana adds texture and flavor, as well as potassium for electrolyte boost, prebiotic fiber for gut health, and a good amount of B6, which supports serotonin production while promoting adrenal support! Now before you go calling the "Keto Police" on me, check out my thoughts on ketosis as a metabolic state, not a food, on page 32.

Makes: 12 muffins | **Prep time:** 10 minutes | **Cook time:** 22 to 25 minutes

6 medium eggs or 5 small eggs

¼ cup ghee, melted and slightly cooled

2 tablespoons coconut oil, melted and slightly cooled

1 banana, mashed

1 cup almond flour

1 heaping tablespoon coconut flour

1½ scoops collagen peptides (12 grams)

½ teaspoon baking soda

1 teaspoon ground cinnamon

1 tablespoon almond extract

1 packed cup grated zucchini

1. Preheat the oven to 375°F.

2. Whisk the eggs with ghee and coconut oil in a large bowl. Mix in the mashed banana.

3. In a medium bowl, mix the almond flour, coconut flour, collagen, baking soda, and cinnamon.

4. Add the dry ingredients to the wet ones, stir until combined, then add the almond extract.

5. Using a cheesecloth or dish towel, press out the remaining water from the shredded zucchini. Then fold the zucchini into the muffin mixture.

6. Line a muffin tin with unbleached muffin liners and scoop ⅛-cup portions into each.

7. Bake for 22 to 25 minutes until a toothpick or knife inserted in the middle of a muffin comes out clean.

Note: If you have not yet tested ghee in your diet, you may sub it out for melted coconut oil or coconut butter.

Nutrition facts per muffin

Calories: 166 | **Carbohydrates:** 6g | **Fiber:** 2g | **Protein:** 6g | **Fat:** 13g

Coconut Cacao Chia Seed Pudding (ef)

FOOD AS MEDICINE   When going low carb, fiber (the healthy non-digestible part of carbs) is often reduced in the diet as well. Over time, a low-fiber diet can have a negative influence on gut health and detoxification as it functions as a prebiotic, feeding the microbiome, and contributes to bowel mass to support regularity. Chia seeds, a whopping 90 percent fiber, stabilize blood sugar levels and maintain energy levels. This recipe yields 20 grams of carbs with 13 grams of fiber per serving—amounts that will likely still keep you fat-fueled and in ketosis while reaping the hormonal balancing and microbiome boost.

Makes: 4 servings | **Prep time:** 5 to 10 minutes | **Set time:** 6 to 8 hours

1 cup full-fat coconut milk

1 cup additive-free almond milk

3 tablespoons cacao powder

1 teaspoon vanilla extract

2 dates, pitted and chopped

3 tablespoons collagen peptides

¼ cup macadamia nuts

½ cup chia seeds

⅛ cup large coconut shreds, to serve

1. Combine the coconut milk, almond milk, cacao, vanilla, dates, collagen, and macadamia nuts in a blender. Run for 1 to 2 minutes until well combined and creamy, then pour in the chia seeds and pulse 2 to 3 times or run on low for 10 seconds.

2. Divide the mixture into 4 ramekins or mason jars and refrigerate for 6 to 8 hours or overnight.

3. Top with coconut shreds prior to serving.

Nutrition facts per serving

Calories: 355 | Carbohydrates: 20g | Fiber: 14g | Protein: 10g | Fat: 27g

Avocado Pudding (nf) (ef)

FOOD AS MEDICINE   This breakfast pudding is a fat-fueled boost to start the day. If making with children, let them sprinkle on their toppings. You may also consider a drizzle of honey on top if you are not doing keto or your carb allotment allows it. Avocado provides mood-stabilizing B vitamins, plus an abundance of folate, which supports methylation. This unique fruit also supports heart health as it is rich in monounsaturated fats and fiber to regulate blood lipids.

Makes: 4 servings | **Prep time:** 10 minutes | **Set time:** 2-plus hours

1½ cups full-fat coconut milk

1½ packed cups mashed avocados (about 2 medium)

2 teaspoons orange zest

2 teaspoons lemon zest

1 tablespoon raw unfiltered honey

1½ tablespoons freshly squeezed lemon juice

2 scoops collagen peptides (16 grams)

1 teaspoon gelatin

1 tablespoon goji berries, to serve

2 tablespoons hemp seeds, to serve

2 tablespoons coconut shreds, to serve

4 kumquats, thinly sliced,* to serve

1. In a blender, combine the coconut milk, avocados, orange and lemon zests, honey, lemon juice, collagen peptides, and gelatin, and mix on medium, scraping down sides if needed, for 60 to 90 seconds, until creamy.

2. Let the mixture sit for 3 to 4 minutes in the blender to allow the gelatin to bloom, then blend on high for 45 seconds.

3. Pour the mixture into 4 bowls and place them in the refrigerator to set for at least 2 hours.

4. When ready to serve, top each bowl with goji berries, hemp seeds, coconut shreds, and kumquat slices.

* If kumquats are unavailable, substitute with 4 teaspoons orange zest.

Nutrition facts per serving

Calories: 372 | **Carbohydrates:** 17g | **Fiber:** 7g | **Protein:** 19g | **Fat:** 27g

To reduce total carbs by 3g per serving, omit honey.

Chapter 4

Salads

Mellow Mama Fennel Salad   (nf) (ef)

FOOD AS MEDICINE Inspired by green goddess dressing, this salad will channel your inner mellow mama! Avocados are a great source of vitamins E, K, and B6, as well as folate. The combination of B vitamins and fatty acids helps manage the stress response and reduce excess cortisol (the stress hormone). Tahini adds a creaminess and a boost of minerals, including magnesium and calcium for relaxation. Tahini can also be used as a source of seed cycling—sesame seed is recommended at the second half of menstruation to promote progesterone surge. The brightness from just a hint of green apple balances out the flavor and adds a delicate tangy sweetness without burning through your carb budget.

Makes: 4 servings | Prep time: 10 to 15 minutes

1 large head butter lettuce, torn into pieces (about 6 cups)

½ cup Mellow Mama Dressing (page 141)

½ cup chopped celery

1 small fennel bulb, thinly sliced (about ⅓ cup)

fennel fronds, chopped (about ⅛ cup)

½ green apple, cut into thin matchsticks

¼ cup roughly chopped parsley leaves

1. Place the butter lettuce in a large bowl and toss with the Mellow Mama Dressing until well coated.

2. Add the celery, fennel bulb and half the fronds, apple, and parsley to the lettuce, and toss to blend flavors.

3. Divide onto four plates and top with remaining chopped fennel fronds.

Nutrition facts per serving

Calories: 235 | Carbohydrates: 14g | Fiber: 5g | Protein: 8g | Fat: 17g

Summer Salad with Pickled Onion (nf) (ef)

FOOD AS MEDICINE   This is my favorite summer side salad. The lime's brightness is balanced out with pungent garlic and cumin. Pickled onions are a source of probiotics. This combination of ingredients provides hormone support with zinc to aid in estrogen metabolism and support hormone production. Cilantro and cumin are powerhouse seasonings that support chelation of toxic metals.

Makes: 4 servings | **Prep time:** 10 to 15 minutes

⅓ cup olive oil

zest of 1 lime

¼ cup freshly squeezed lime juice (from 2 to 3 limes)

1 clove garlic, finely minced

1 teaspoon ground cumin

1 teaspoon honey

¼ teaspoon salt

10 cups leafy greens

½ cup pickled onions

¼ cup pepitas

1 avocado, cubed

½ cup cilantro leaves, chopped

¼ teaspoon coarse salt

1. Place the olive oil, lime zest, lime juice, garlic, cumin, honey, and salt in a jar with a lid, then shake vigorously for about 2 minutes to emulsify.

2. In a large bowl, toss the greens and remaining ingredients with the dressing. Serve 2 to 3 cups on each plate and top with coarse salt.

Nutrition facts per serving

Calories: 300 | Carbohydrates: 11g | Fiber: 5g | Protein: 5g | Fat: 28g

Kale Salad with Squash and Pomegranate (ef)

FOOD AS MEDICINE   Squash may be seen as the forbidden fruit of the ketogenic diet; however, with my whole-food approach, your body's individual metabolic processes and state of insulin resistance will determine whether this works for you. If necessary, consider halving the amount of squash to still get its serotonin boost, which supports mood without kicking you out of fat-burning mode. The cinnamon and coconut oil aids in metabolic process. Pomegranate adds epigallocatechin gallate (EGCG), the same antioxidant in green tea that is attributed to many anti-aging and cellular protective mechanisms.

Makes: 4 servings | Prep time: 15 to 20 minutes | Cook time: 35 to 40 minutes

2 delicata squashes, ends cut, deseeded, and cut into ½-inch slices

1 tablespoon melted coconut oil

1 tablespoon avocado oil

½ teaspoon ground cinnamon

½ teaspoon coarse salt

½ cup raw pecan halves

1 large bunch lacinato kale, stemmed and cut into thin ribbons

¼ cup extra-virgin olive oil

¼ cup apple cider vinegar

1 teaspoon robust, dark amber maple syrup

½ teaspoon freshly ground black pepper

¼ cup pomegranate seeds

1 avocado, sliced

1. Preheat the oven to 375°F.

2. Arrange the squash in a single layer on a baking sheet.

3. Drizzle the melted coconut oil and avocado oil over the squash, tossing to coat until all of the pieces are glistening. Sprinkle with the cinnamon and coarse salt.

4. Bake for 20 minutes, then shake or scrape the squash with a spatula to mix and flip the pieces so they brown evenly.

5. Place the raw pecan halves on a separate baking sheet in the middle of the oven and roast for about 15 minutes, until aromatic and lightly roasted. On the lower rack, return the squash to the oven for another 5 to 10 minutes. Remove and let sit for 5 minutes.

6. While the squash is roasting, place the kale in a large salad bowl and massage the pieces with your hands to break down the dense plant for about 30 to 45 seconds.

7. In a separate bowl, whisk together the olive oil, apple cider vinegar, maple syrup, and pepper.

8. Toss the dressing over the kale and add the roasted squash, pecans, and pomegranate seeds to coat and combine.

9. Serve the salad mixture with 2 to 3 slices avocado, about ¼ avocado each.

Nutrition facts per serving

Calories: 398 | Carbohydrates: 14g | Fiber: 7g | Protein: 4g | Fat: 39g

Hemp Jalapeño Cabbage Slaw

(nf)

FOOD AS MEDICINE   Slaw is a great way to take in the dense fibers of cabbage while minimizing the bitter, sulfurous taste of the beneficial indole-3-carbinol that drives detoxification. This slaw pairs perfectly with a summer BBQ or fish tacos, with brightness from the lime and a spicy kick from the jalapeño. Cabbage has very low calorie density yet is packed with vitamin C to regulate adrenal gland health, and prebiotic fiber for "feel good" lactobacillus and bifido bacteria strains to thrive on. The creamy mayo is warmed with cumin, a seasoning that's rich in glutathione to boost antioxidant capacity in the body, and enhanced with the pungent antioxidant boost in fresh garlic. Top it with hemp seeds to round out the flavors and add a nice crunch. This slaw is a showstopper; bring it to your next gathering and guests will talk about it.

Makes: 4 servings | Prep time: 10 to 15 minutes

4 cups thinly sliced red cabbage

2 cups thinly sliced green cabbage, 7 to 8 full leaves reserved

1 teaspoon salt, divided

2 leaves lacinato kale, cut into thin ribbons

2 cloves garlic, finely minced

juice of 3 limes (about 3 tablespoons)

½ cup avocado oil mayonnaise

½ cup chopped cilantro

1 teaspoon ground cumin

2 tablespoons hemp seeds

2 tablespoons thinly sliced fresh jalapeño

¼ cup jicama, sliced into matchsticks about ⅛ inch by 1 inch

1. Sprinkle the sliced cabbage with ½ teaspoon salt and massage for 75 to 90 seconds to break down the dense leaves. In the last 15 seconds or so, sprinkle in the kale and continue to massage lightly, breaking down kale.

2. In a separate bowl, mix the garlic, lime juice, remaining ½ teaspoon salt, mayonnaise, cilantro, and cumin until well combined.

3. Pour the dressing over the slaw, stirring to coat.

4. Top with hemp seeds, jalapeño, and jicama.

Nutrition facts per serving
Calories: 266 | Carbohydrates: 13g | Fiber: 5g | Protein: 4g | Fat: 23g

Farmer's Market Salad

FOOD AS MEDICINE   Combining acid and fat, such as lemon with olive oil, aids in nutrient absorption. Greens are a great source of mood-stabilizing nutrients, including folate and magnesium. Choose heirloom varieties and local heads for more nutrient density.

Makes: 4 servings | **Prep time:** 15 minutes

1 small head heirloom lettuce such as Deer Tongue, Speckled Trout, or May Queen

2 handfuls arugula

3 tablespoons freshly squeezed lemon juice

3 tablespoons extra-virgin olive oil

½ teaspoon honey

generous pinch of salt

9 to 10 twists freshly ground black pepper

8 to 10 slices watermelon radish

8 to 10 fresh edible flowers

1 teaspoon large flake sea salt, such as Maldon

1. Place the lettuce and arugula in a large bowl.

2. In a small bowl, whisk the lemon juice, olive oil, honey, salt, and pepper. Pour over leafy greens and toss to coat evenly.

3. Top the dressed greens with the radish, edible flowers, and a sprinkle of salt.

Nutrition facts per serving

Calories: 161 | Carbohydrates: 2g | Fiber: 1g | Protein: 2g | Fat: 15g

Sardine Caesar Salad

(nf)

FOOD AS MEDICINE   It's important to eat wild-caught fish three times a week for anti-inflammatory support from omega-3 fatty acids, yet this can get somewhat mundane if you don't mix it up. Reminiscent of a classic Caesar, this salad contains olive oil and egg to provide hormone-building, brain-boosting nutrients, but leaves out the breadcrumbs and other inflammatory, processed additives. Many people dislike sardines, but these little fish are strongly recommended for their calcium-rich bones. Calcium is an anti-anxiety mineral that aids in mellowing out the neuromuscular system while supporting structural health. When you blend the sardines into the dressing, it adds creaminess and nutrient density without the texture of fish bones.

Makes: 4 servings | **Prep time:** 10 to 15 minutes

¼ cup smoked sardines

juice of 1 lemon (about ¼ cup)

zest of 1 lemon, divided

1 teaspoon Dijon mustard

¼ teaspoon salt

½ teaspoon freshly ground black pepper

1 clove garlic, smashed

1 room-temperature egg

¼ cup olive oil

1 large head of romaine lettuce, cored and chopped (about 8 cups)

4 servings Stella's Simple Wild Salmon (page 106)

1. In a blender, combine the sardines, lemon juice, all but 1 teaspoon of lemon zest, mustard, salt, pepper, and garlic and blend on high until well combined.

2. While the motor is running, add the egg, then the olive oil until emulsified.

3. Divide the romaine onto four plates and place a piece of salmon on each. Drizzle with the dressing and garnish with the remaining lemon zest.

Nutrition facts per serving

Calories: 385 | **Carbohydrates:** 9g | **Fiber:** 3g | **Protein:** 35g | **Fat:** 25g

Rustic Balsamic and Vegetable Salad (ef)

FOOD AS MEDICINE   Salads are a vehicle for flavor, fat, and antioxidants. The rustic, robust flavors of balsamic vinegar and fresh herbs with the crunchy kick of pungent truffle complements crispy roasted veggies. Cauliflower and Brussels sprouts provide a boost of glutathione and indole-3-carbinol (I3C) to reduce inflammation, support liver health, drive detoxification, and reduce free radicals in the body.

Makes: 6 servings | Prep time: 10 to 15 minutes | Cook time: 30 to 35 minutes

1 head cauliflower, cored and cut into 1- to 2-inch pieces (about 3 cups)

3 cups quartered Brussels sprouts (from about 5 cups whole Brussels sprouts)

3 tablespoons avocado oil

1 teaspoon salt

2 tablespoons roughly chopped fresh thyme leaves

10 to 12 cups salad greens

½ cup Rustic Balsamic Dressing (page 140)

½ cup Truffled Rosemary Marcona Almonds (page 125), chopped

1. Preheat the oven to 400°F.

2. Spread the cauliflower on a baking sheet and the Brussels sprouts on another.

3. Drizzle the avocado oil over both baking sheets equally and toss the vegetables to coat until all of the pieces are glistening.

4. Sprinkle the salt and thyme over the cauliflower and Brussels sprouts, tossing to evenly distribute.

5. Place both baking sheets in the oven with the Brussels sprouts on the bottom rack. Bake for 22 minutes, then shake or scrape both trays with a spatula to mix and shift the vegetables so they brown evenly.

6. Return the trays to the oven for another 8 to 12 minutes, depending on your desired crispiness.

7. While the vegetables are roasting, toss the salad greens and Rustic Balsamic Dressing in a large bowl.

8. When the vegetables are done roasting, let them sit for 2 minutes, then toss with fresh thyme and incorporate into the dressed salad mix. Top with chopped almonds and serve immediately.

Nutrition facts per serving

Calories: 312 | Carbohydrates: 13g | Fiber: 4g | Protein: 9g | Fat: 25g

Antipasto Salad

FOOD AS MEDICINE This salad satisfies all cravings for an Italian sandwich without the gluten, inflammation, or gut distress. The briny olives and bright acidity in the red wine vinegar creates a contrast to the fat-marbled salami. Artichokes have prebiotic fiber and diuretic effects that support detoxification. The light butter lettuce contrasts well with the hearty kale, which creates a denser base for all the add-ins.

Makes: 4 servings | **Prep time:** 10 to 15 minutes

2 cups lacinato kale, stemmed and chopped

3 cups butter lettuce, cored and chopped

1 cup chopped cucumber

3 tablespoons diced red onion

1 cup sliced red bell pepper

½ cup pitted chopped kalamata olives

⅔ cup chopped artichoke hearts

4 ounces salami, chopped

¼ cup chopped fresh parsley

⅓ cup red wine vinegar

⅓ cup olive oil

½ teaspoon freshly ground black pepper

¼ teaspoon salt

½ teaspoon coarse flake salt

1. Place the kale in a large salad bowl and massage the pieces with your hands to break down the dense plant fibers. Sprinkle with salt and twist the leaves in your hands for about 30 to 45 seconds.

2. Add the lettuce, cucumber, onion, bell pepper, olives, artichoke hearts, and salami.

3. In a 12-ounce or larger jar with a lid, combine the parsley, vinegar, olive oil, black pepper, and salt. Shake for 3 minutes until the oil and vinegar are well blended.

4. Pour the dressing over the salad and toss to combine. Top with coarse salt and serve.

Nutrition facts per serving

Calories: 345 | Carbohydrates: 13g | Fiber: 4g | Protein: 8g | Fat: 29g

Golden Lemon Zinger with Coconut Pistachios and Shrimp

(ef)

FOOD AS MEDICINE Lemon is my go-to acid when blending flavors, especially when I'm creating recipes for clients who are maintaining a vinegar-free diet during a microbiome cleanse. The bright, vitamin C–rich boost of lemon is complemented with anti-inflammatory turmeric and ginger in the salad dressing. This light but robustly flavored dish is enhanced with omega-3 and selenium-rich shrimp. Large coconut flakes play on the warming curry of the dressing while providing fat-burning and ketone-producing MCTs.

Makes: 4 servings | **Prep time:** 10 to 15 minutes | **Cook time:** 8 to 10 minutes

1 tablespoon avocado oil

1 tablespoon coconut oil

1 pound large wild-caught shrimp

½ teaspoon salt

½ teaspoon freshly ground black pepper

2 tablespoons chopped scallions greens

10 to 12 cups salad mix

1½ cups Golden Lemon Zinger Dressing (page 140)

⅓ cup pistachios

¼ cup toasted coconut flakes

1. Heat a 12-inch cast-iron skillet on medium-high, then add the avocado and coconut oils.

2. Once the oils are melted, add the shrimp and stir to coat, then add in the salt and pepper and stir.

3. Cook the shrimp for 3 to 4 minutes undisturbed, then stir again, flipping to the other side and cooking another 3 to 4 minutes until pink throughout. Set aside.

4. In a large bowl, add the scallions, salad greens, Golden Lemon Zinger Dressing, pistachios, and coconut flakes, tossing between each addition.

5. Divide the salad onto four plates and top each plate with 4 to 6 shrimp.

Nutrition facts per serving

Calories: 545 | **Carbohydrates:** 15g | **Fiber:** 5g | **Protein:** 33g | **Fat:** 40g

Chapter 5

Soups

Cream of Kale Soup with Crispy Prosciutto Chips (nf) (ef)

FOOD AS MEDICINE Broth and kale are each superfoods in their own right. Bone broth is rich in glycine, which supports neuromuscular relaxation and GABA expression in the brain while providing glutamine and gelatin for gut health. Kale is an anti-inflammatory and detoxifying leafy green rich in isothiocyanates (ITCs), which play a role in anti-aging by supporting the body's detoxification process at the genetic level.

Makes: 4 servings | **Prep time:** 15 minutes | **Cook time:** 40 to 45 minutes

2 tablespoons olive oil

½ large yellow onion, chopped (about 1 heaping cup)

½ teaspoon salt

⅛ teaspoon white pepper

2 cloves garlic, minced (about 1 heaping tablespoon)

1 bunch lacinato kale, stemmed (about 3 packed cups)

6 cups chicken bone broth

⅓ cup full-fat coconut milk

½ teaspoon freshly ground black pepper

4 ounces prosciutto, cut into 2 x 3-inch pieces

1. Preheat the oven to 400°F.

2. Heat a large stock pot over medium-high, then add the olive oil, onion, salt, and white pepper. Stir to coat and combine, then reduce the heat to medium. Cook for about 10 minutes, until the onions are soft and caramelized, stirring only once every 2 to 3 minutes. About halfway through, stir in the garlic.

3. Add the kale and sauté about 2-minutes until it cooks down and softens, then add the chicken bone broth. As the liquid starts to simmer, reduce the heat to low, cover, and cook for 10 to 12 minutes.

4. Add the coconut milk and stir to combine. Use an immersion blender to puree the soup in the pot or transfer to a blender in batches to blend and return to the pot. Add the black pepper and stir to combine. Simmer uncovered

for an additional 10 to 15 minutes to thicken, stirring every 3 to 4 minutes.

5. As the soup is simmering, place the prosciutto on a baking sheet in the middle rack of the oven and bake for 10 minutes, checking at 8 minutes and shaking the pan. Remove the pan from the oven once the prosciutto starts to curl at the ends and is crispy like chips.

6. Ladle 2½ cups of soup into each bowl and top with 2 to 3 prosciutto chips. Serve with additional cracked black pepper on top, if desired.

Nutrition facts per serving

Calories: 150 | Carbohydrates: 2g | Fiber: 1g | Protein: 11g | Fat: 10g

Zesty Creamy Carrot Soup (nf) (ef)

FOOD AS MEDICINE This soup pairs a base of nourishing bone broth with antioxidant-rich carrots. I don't peel organic root vegetables so they retain the soil-based minerals and microbes for healthy gut bacteria support. Carrots are also a great source of vitamins A, K, and C. This soup has a nice zing from anti-inflammatory and digestion-supporting ginger.

Makes: 6 (1½ cup) servings | Prep time: 30 to 40 minutes | Cook time: 35 to 40 minutes

2 tablespoons coconut oil

1 yellow onion, chopped

2 teaspoons sea salt, divided, plus more to taste

1½ cups carrots, chopped into 1-inch pieces

6 cups chicken bone broth

3 inches ginger, peeled and roughly chopped

juice and zest of 1 orange

1 (13.5-ounce) can full-fat coconut milk

Himalayan pink salt, to taste

freshly ground black pepper, to taste, plus more for garnish

chopped fresh mint and basil, for garnish

1. Add the coconut oil to a stock pot over medium-high heat. When the oil is melted, add the onion and 1 teaspoon sea salt, stirring to coat. Cook the onion undisturbed for 3 to 4 minutes, stir, and let sit for another 3 to 4 minutes until it is soft and golden brown.

2. Add the carrots and remaining teaspoon of sea salt, stirring to coat. Cook for about 4 to 5 minutes, then add the broth and ginger, cover, and simmer for 20 minutes.

3. Stir the orange juice and zest into the soup. Continue to cook uncovered for 3 to 5 minutes. Add the coconut milk and season with salt and pepper to taste, then simmer for a few more minutes for the flavors to combine.

4. Puree to a velvety texture, either working in batches in a standing blender, or directly in the pot using an immersion blender.

5. Serve with chopped mint, basil, and freshly ground black pepper.

Nutrition facts per serving

Calories: 125 | Carbohydrates: 6g | Fiber: 1g | Protein: 12g | Fat: 6g

Dashi Broth Soup with Seaweed (nf) (ef)

FOOD AS MEDICINE   The umami base for savory Japanese dishes, traditional dashi is made by adding kombu or bonito to water, which produces a light fishy flavor. But this recipe uses bone broth, which packs in more nutrient density with glycine, gelatin, and glutamine to support stress response and a mellow mood. I also find the poultry flavor base and earthy dried shiitakes add complexity and cut some of the fishy flavor, as well as provide more therapeutic ingredients to support thyroid and immune health. This dish uses large-flake white fish for a quick and easy weeknight protein that you can divide into batches once the broth is made, adding the fish to each serving when reheating.

Makes: 6 (1½ cup) servings | **Prep time:** 5 to 10 minutes | **Cook time:** 40 to 45 minutes

6 cups chicken or turkey bone broth

3 (1 x 4-inch) strips kombu

1½ cups dried or 3 cups fresh shiitake mushrooms

½ cup bonito flakes (I used Eden brand)

2 (6-ounce) wild-caught halibut or other white fish fillets

⅛ cup scallions, green parts chopped

3 tablespoons miso (optional)

1. Heat the turkey or chicken bone broth in a medium pot over medium-high heat.

2. Once the broth is simmering, break the kombu strips in half and add them to the broth along with the dried shiitake mushrooms (fresh ones are added later in the process). Simmer for 15 to 20 minutes, until the kombu and mushrooms are softened.

3. Add the bonito flakes and simmer an additional 5 to 10 minutes.

4. Remove from heat and strain the broth. Pick out the shiitakes and trim off the woody ends of the stems, then slice the caps. Discard the stem ends, kombu, and bonito residue.

5. Return the broth and sliced shiitakes to pot and simmer on low until softened, about 8 to 10 minutes. If you are using fresh shiitakes, add them now.

6. Add the halibut and simmer on low for another 4 to 5 minutes, until cooked through.

7. Turn off the heat and stir in the scallions and miso, if using.*

If you have advanced your anti-anxiety diet to reintroduce and tolerate organic miso, a health-supporting, probiotic-rich fermented food, you may serve by stirring 1 to 2 teaspoons miso into each portion.

Nutrition facts per serving

Calories: 228 | **Carbohydrates:** 13g | **Fiber:** 4g | **Protein:** 41g | **Fat:** 5g

Creamy Green Chili Chicken Soup (nf) (ef)

FOOD AS MEDICINE   The capsaicin in Hatch chiles will not only kick up some heat in your belly but also support metabolism. Avocado cools things down while providing a source of potassium, B vitamins, and fiber. The jicama is a potent prebiotic fiber that fuels good bacteria for healthy growth of probiotics and a symbiotic gut. The prebiotics in this soup are further supported with bone broth, which protects and lines the GI tract and promotes relaxation.

Makes: 8 (1½ cup) servings | **Prep time:** 10 to 15 minutes | **Cook time:** 35 to 40 minutes

1½ tablespoons avocado oil

1 red onion, chopped

3 cloves garlic, crushed

2 tablespoons ground cumin

1 yellow bell pepper, chopped

1 teaspoon sea salt

2 cups medium-heat canned, jarred, or frozen Hatch chiles

8 cups chicken bone broth

1¼ cups full-fat coconut milk

3 avocados, divided

1 cup chopped jicama, divided

2 cups shredded rotisserie chicken

1 bunch cilantro, leaves chopped

1. Add the avocado oil to a large stock pot over medium-high heat. Add the onion and sauté until softened, 4 to 5 minutes.

2. Add the garlic and cumin, stirring to combine. Add the bell pepper and reduce heat to medium, season with sea salt, and sauté until softened, 4 to 5 minutes.

3. Add the Hatch chiles and bone broth, stirring to combine. Increase heat to medium-high to bring to a low boil, then reduce to a simmer.

4. Once simmering, add the coconut milk and allow the soup to thicken slightly, about 10 minutes.

5. Puree two-thirds of the soup in a blender in two batches. In each batch, add 1 avocado and ¼ cup jicama, blending on high. (Hold a towel over blender top when blending hot liquids to prevent burns.) This creates a mostly creamy soup with some texture from the unblended soup left in the stock pot.

6. Return the pureed soup to the stock pot and stir to combine. Add the shredded chicken. Bring back to a simmer for 4 to 5 minutes to allow the flavors to meld.

7. Ladle into soup bowls and top with 2 tablespoons each of chopped avocado, jicama, and cilantro.

Nutrition facts per serving

Calories: 275 | **Carbohydrates:** 12g | **Fiber:** 5g | **Protein:** 16g | **Fat:** 20g

Thai Green Curry Chicken Soup (nf) (ef)

FOOD AS MEDICINE   I am a huge fan of Thai food, so coming up with an option that was soy-free, gluten-free, and free of additives and preservatives was essential in my whole-food transition. This recipe has all the flavor and antioxidants without any of the gunk. It's also rich in vegetables, with kale added at the end of the process. I like to top with kimchi sriracha for an added probiotic boost, or you may decide to stay traditional and chop up a spicy Thai chili.

Makes: 8 (1½ cup) servings | Prep time: 10 to 15 minutes | Cook time: 50 to 60 minutes

2 tablespoons coconut oil

½ red onion, chopped

2 inches fresh ginger, minced (about 1 tablespoon)

1 inch fresh turmeric, skin on and finely chopped (about 1 tablespoon)

2 stalks lemongrass, halved and sliced vertically

8 cups bone broth (this recipe is great with a 50/50 mix of chicken and beef bone broth)

3 tablespoons green curry paste, such as Thai Kitchen

1 (13.5-ounce) can full-fat coconut milk

1 cup water or broth

2 to 3 stalks chopped celery (about 2 cups)

1 bunch kale, stemmed and finely chopped (about 4 cups)

3 carrots (about ¾ cup), chopped into ¼-inch-thick coins

1 rotisserie chicken, skinned, deboned, and shredded

1 tablespoon fish sauce

1 orange bell pepper, thinly sliced (about 1½ cups)

1 bunch cilantro, stemmed and leaves chopped (about 2 cups)

1 bunch mint, stemmed and leaves chopped (about ¼ cup)

1 to 3 teaspoons fermented sriracha, such as Wildbrine Probiotic Spicy Kimchi Sriracha, to serve (optional)

1. Add the coconut oil to a 10- to 12-quart stock pot over medium-high heat.

2. Sauté the onion, ginger, and turmeric for 3 to 5 minutes, stirring infrequently to allow for some browning.

3. Stir the onion mixture once more and add half the lemongrass pieces, smashing them prior to adding to the pot. Reduce the heat to medium-low and stir another 4 to 5 minutes until the onion and herbs are caramelized and start to form a light brown crust at the bottom of the pan.

4. Add the bone broth, scraping up the browned pieces on the bottom of the pan. Whisk in the green curry paste, then simmer for 10 minutes until reduced. Reduce the heat if needed to avoid boiling.

5. Remove the lemongrass and discard.

6. Puree the soup with an immersion blender or in a stand-up blender and return it to the pot.

7. Add the remaining sliced lemongrass to the soup, without smashing, along with the coconut milk, water or broth, and celery. Simmer for 15 minutes.

8. Add the kale and carrots and simmer 10 minutes.

9. Add the rotisserie chicken, fish sauce, and bell peppers, reduce the heat to low, and simmer for 10 minutes.

10. Remove the lemongrass and serve in bowls with 2 tablespoons chopped cilantro and mint each. Top with sriracha, if desired.

Nutrition facts per serving

Calories: 411 | Carbohydrates: 12g | Fiber: 3g | Protein: 38g | Fat: 19g

Roasted Red Pepper Bisque

(ef)

FOOD AS MEDICINE   This is a velvety bowl of yum—charred red bell peppers complement the meaty broth while the pesto provides an awesome pop of brightness and boosts the soup's vitamin C to the next level! Peppers are also a rich source of vitamin C, which reduces oxidative stress and is used by the adrenal glands in cortisol metabolism. Red bell peppers provide natural sweetness to tame sugar cravings and boost B6 to reduce stress with serotonin and dopamine production. They are also rich in carotenoids and other polyphenols that reduce inflammation in the body. Studies have shown that eating bell peppers and bell pepper extracts can lower blood sugar levels, drive bile flow, and support detoxification and cholesterol-lowering effects.

Makes: 6 (1½ cup) servings | Prep time: 20 to 25 minutes | Cook time: 30 to 35 minutes

3 red bell peppers

2 tablespoons olive oil

1 yellow onion, chopped (about 2 cups)

1 teaspoon salt

2 small carrots, chopped (about ½ cup)

3 cloves garlic, finely chopped
(about 1 heaping tablespoon)

1 (14.5-ounce) can diced tomatoes, drained

3 cups beef bone broth

2 tablespoons roughly chopped fresh thyme leaves

¾ teaspoon freshly ground black pepper

⅔ cup Simple Kale Pesto (page 138), to serve

⅛ cup pine nuts, to serve

1. Roast the red peppers (see instructions below) and chop them up.

2. While the peppers are roasting, heat a large pan over medium heat. Once warm, add the olive oil, onion, and salt, stirring to coat in oil. Cook for 5 to 6 minutes, stirring every 2 minutes.

3. Add the carrots and garlic, stirring to coat and combine. Cook for another 5 to 6 minutes, stirring every 2 to 3 minutes until the vegetables start to stick.

4. Add the red peppers and tomatoes, stirring to combine. Simmer for 3 to 4 minutes, then add the beef bone broth, stirring to loosen up the vegetables and reduce the browning. Return to a simmer and then reduce the heat to low.

5. Add the thyme leaves and black pepper.

6. Simmer on low for 15 to 20 minutes, then puree with an immersion blender or transfer in batches to a blender. After blending, return to the stove top and simmer for another 5 to 10 minutes to combine the flavors.

7. Serve topped with 2 to 3 tablespoons of Simple Kale Pesto and pine nuts.

Note: Vitamin C and other antioxidant levels are 10% to 30% higher in concentration in organically grown foods. Since they are included in the Dirty Dozen (see page 36), purchase organic bell peppers both for more nutrition and for less toxicity to the body and neurological system.

Note: Although peppers have many favorable impacts, they are in the nightshade family and, if you are dealing with autoimmune disease–related inflammation, it may be worth eliminating nightshades for three months to see if they are contributing to your symptoms.

Nutrition facts per serving

Calories: 313 | Carbohydrates: 16g | Fiber: 5g | Protein: 19g | Fat: 21g

Roasting Red Peppers

For the most flavorful roasted red peppers, place cleaned whole peppers over an open flame, such as an outdoor grill, a stove top gas burner, or on a baking sheet in the oven directly under the broiler flame. Turn every 4 to 5 minutes for a total of about 4 rotations. Remove the peppers from the heat, place them on a flat surface (such as a cutting board), and cover with a bowl to steam and cook through. This also makes it easier to remove the skin. You can also place them in an airtight container such as a sealable glass container to achieve the same results. When cooled, remove skin, stem, and seeds.

Anti-Anxiety Diet Bone Broth

(nf) (nf)

FOOD AS MEDICINE Bone broth is a top food as medicine; it works as an expectorant to break up mucus and phlegm and boosts supportive connective tissue and gut health. Making this a staple in your diet will aid in immune and anti-inflammatory support for whole-body health while promoting GABA to reduce anxiety and impulse. Drink in a mug, use as a broth to deglaze pans after sautéing veggies, or use as a soup base. The addition of kombu and butternut squash enhances the mood-stabilizing properties by promoting serotonin expression. The light floral chamomile and rosemary nicely offset the savory flavor while promoting relaxation and memory.

Makes: 8 (10-ounce) servings | Prep time: 10 to 15 minutes | Cook time: 24 to 36 hours

1 roasted chicken carcass

1 tablespoon sea salt

2 tablespoons black peppercorns

2 (4-inch) strips kombu

1 yellow onion with skin, roughly chopped

½ red onion with skin, roughly chopped

1 cup butternut squash, peeled and cubed

4 large rainbow carrots, chopped in 2- to 3-inch pieces (about 2 cups)

1 bunch carrot tops

½ bunch celery, leaves on, chopped (about 2 cups)

3 sprigs fresh rosemary

12 cups water

8 to 9 cloves garlic, skinned and smashed

1 to 3 cups vegetable scraps (onion skins, chard stems, carrot tops, etc.)

2 teaspoons ground turmeric

3 bay leaves

2 teaspoons organic raw unfiltered apple cider vinegar

2 tablespoons chamomile tea

1. Add all of the ingredients except for the chamomile tea in a 10-quart or larger stock pot over high heat and bring to a boil. Once boiling, reduce heat to low, cover, and simmer for 24 to 36 hours.

2. In the last 30 minutes of simmering, stir in the chamomile tea.

3. Strain, discard the solids, and pour the broth into glass jars.

4. Cool uncovered at room temperature for about 20 minutes. Cover and refrigerate until chilled below 50°F. Broth will keep for 5 to 7 days in the refrigerator or 8 to 12 months in the freezer.

Note: Pour extra broth into ice cube trays and freeze. Use cubes to sauté with vegetables or to heat up an individual mug of bone broth.

Nutrition facts per serving

Calories: 73 | Carbohydrates: 1g | Fiber: 0g | Protein: 6g | Fat: 5g

Chapter 6

Vegetables

Savory Ranch Kale Chips (nf)(ef)

FOOD AS MEDICINE When looking for a salty, crunchy snack on a low-carb, dairy-free diet, choices may be limited. Kale chips are a great way to fill up while providing vitamins K, A, and C as well as magnesium, calcium, and microbiome-supportive fiber. The flavonoids and phytocompounds in kale such as kaempferol and lutein reduce inflammation and support detoxification processes, making this a superfood replacement for your typical snack.

Makes: 4 servings | Prep time: 5 minutes | Cook time: 15 to 20 minutes

1 bunch curly kale, stemmed and torn into 2-inch pieces (about 5 cups)

2 teaspoons olive oil

2 teaspoons avocado oil

½ teaspoon dried parsley

¼ teaspoon onion powder

¼ teaspoon garlic powder

½ teaspoon dried dill

½ teaspoon sea salt

1. Preheat the oven to 300°F. Line a baking sheet with parchment paper.

2. Place the kale in a large bowl and pour in the oils, massaging with your hands until all of the pieces are covered and glistening.

3. In a small bowl, combine the remaining ingredients. Sprinkle the mixture over the kale and stir to distribute.

4. Spread the kale in a single layer on the baking sheet. Do not overcrowd as this will steam the kale.

5. Bake in batches for 15 to 20 minutes until crispy.

Note: This recipe is best right out of the oven. The kale chips won't be good beyond 4 hours, but if you're trying to keep longer, store at room temperature.

Nutrition facts per serving

Calories: 83 | **Carbohydrates:** 8g | **Fiber:** 4g | **Protein:** 6g | **Fat:** 5g

Simple Roasted Beets

(nf) (ef)

FOOD AS MEDICINE Beets contain betalain, an antioxidant that reduces lipid oxidation and the production of LDL particles. They also activate Phase 2 detox enzymes, which aid in the encapsulation of toxins. This recipe is a classic example of how my food-as-medicine approach prioritizes nutrient density over macros, adjusting the synergy of the meal to support the metabolic goals of ketosis.

Makes: 4 (⅔-cup) servings | **Prep time:** 10 minutes | **Cook time:** 40 to 45 minutes

3 to 4 medium beets, cut into 1-inch pieces (about 2 to 3 cups)

2 tablespoons avocado oil

¼ teaspoon salt

7 to 8 twists freshly ground black pepper (about ½ teaspoon)

¼ teaspoon coarse salt, to serve

1. Preheat the oven to 375°F.

2. Place the beets on a baking sheet and rub with the avocado oil until all the pieces are glistening.

3. Sprinkle the salt and pepper over the beets and shake the pan to distribute.

4. Roast in the oven for 40 to 45 minutes, checking at 20 minutes to stir and shake before returning to the oven.

5. Once cooked to desired texture, toss the beets into a medium-sized bowl, stirring to combine flavors and tossing with coarse salt prior to serving.

Nutrition facts per serving

Calories: 106 | **Carbohydrates:** 10g | **Fiber:** 4g | **Protein:** 2g | **Fat:** 7g

Braised Greens

(nf) (ef)

FOOD AS MEDICINE Leafy greens are a must in your diet. They are rich in mood-boosting and health-supporting minerals, vitamins, and antioxidants. And when you're craving that feeling of satiety from the stretch receptors in your belly, leafy greens contribute volume with little calorie density, which is important in a fat-dominant diet where calories can quickly add up.

Makes: 4 servings | **Prep time:** 5 minutes | **Cook time:** 20 to 25 minutes

2 tablespoons olive oil

1 yellow onion, thinly sliced

4 cloves garlic, chopped

generous pinch of salt

1 teaspoon ground turmeric

½ cup chicken bone broth

1 bunch rainbow chard, collard greens, or lacinato kale, stems separated from leaves (about 4 to 5 cups)

½ teaspoon red chili flakes

1. Heat a cast-iron or stainless-steel skillet over medium-high heat.

2. Add the olive oil and onion. Stir thoroughly to coat, then let sit for 4 to 5 minutes. Stir once more, then allow to sit for another 3 to 4 minutes.

3. Add the garlic and salt. Stir every minute or so for 2 to 3 minutes.

4. As the garlic and onion are cooking, combine the turmeric and bone broth in a separate small bowl.

5. After 5 minutes, add the leafy greens and pour the bone broth with turmeric into the pan. Coat the greens and allow the bone broth to simmer, wilting greens down to about half the volume.

6. At about 5 to 6 minutes into cooking the greens, sprinkle in the chili flakes to taste, adding more if you like it spicy. Sauté for another 3 to 4 minutes, then turn off the heat and allow to sit for 2 to 3 minutes prior to serving.

Nutrition facts per serving

Calories: 76 | Carbohydrates: 2g | Fiber: 1g | Protein: 1g | Fat: 7g

Roasted Butternut Squash with Coconut Oil and Cinnamon

(nf) (ef)

FOOD AS MEDICINE   Warming seasonings in this recipe reduce inflammation and support healthy blood sugar metabolism while satisfying cravings for pumpkin pie or savory seasonal treats. Butternut squash boosts your mood with a bounty of tryptophan and folate used for serotonin production. The coconut oil coating is a great way to balance and promote hormone rebound in the body. Once you have adapted to fat as your primary fuel when on a low-carb diet, this starchy vegetable provides B vitamins, vitamin E, and electrolyte-supporting potassium. Serve it warm as a side or add to your favorite salad.

Makes: 6 (⅔-cup) servings | **Prep time:** 10 to 15 minutes | **Cook time:** 25 to 30 minutes

5 cups butternut squash, peeled and cubed

2 tablespoons melted coconut oil

2 teaspoons ground cinnamon

½ teaspoon ground ginger

½ teaspoon salt

¼ teaspoon coarse salt, to serve

1. Preheat the oven to 400°F.

2. Place the squash on a baking sheet and toss with the melted coconut oil to coat.

3. In a small bowl, mix together the cinnamon, ginger, and salt. Sprinkle the mixture over the glistening squash.

4. Roast the squash in the middle rack of the oven for 20 to 25 minutes until tender.

5. Once it is cooked to desired softness, turn on the broiler and broil for 2 to 3 minutes for a nice crispy finish.

6. Remove from the pan and toss in a bowl with coarse salt to serve.

Note: If you peel and cube your own butternut squash, save the skin for bone broth.

Nutrition facts per serving

Calories: 95 | **Carbohydrates:** 15g | **Fiber:** 4g | **Protein:** 1g | **Fat:** 5g

Crispy Brussels with Umi Plum Vinegar (nf)(ef)

FOOD AS MEDICINE Brussels sprouts are nutrient-dense balls of flavor that contain sulforaphane compounds that promote anti-inflammatory and detoxification support. Research has shown that this vegetable increases glutathione levels in the body, which supports antioxidant function, protects against free radical damage, and boosts liver health. Umi plum vinegar has a light acidity with a briny brightness that can elevate almost any dish.

Makes: 4 servings | Prep time: 10 to 15 minutes | Cook time: 15 to 20 minutes

4 tablespoons avocado oil

4 cups thinly sliced Brussels sprouts

½ teaspoon salt

1 tablespoon umi plum vinegar

1 tablespoon champagne vinegar

3 tablespoons chopped fresh basil

1 tablespoon chopped fresh mint

1. Preheat the oven to 375°F.

2. In an oven-safe pan over medium heat, add the oil and Brussels sprouts and sauté, stirring frequently to coat evenly with oil. Sprinkle with salt, stir once more, then allow to cook for 3 to 4 minutes until starting to soften. Stir once and place in the oven for about 15 minutes, until sprouts are crispy. If at 15 minutes they are done but don't have a crispy crunch, consider placing under the broiler for 30 to 45 seconds.

3. Once crisped as desired, toss in vinegars and fresh herbs.

Nutrition facts per serving

Calories: 169 | Carbohydrates: 9g | Fiber: 4g | Protein: 3g | Fat: 14g

Cauliflower Pine Nut Salad

(ef)

FOOD AS MEDICINE Cruciferous vegetables are potent detoxifiers and support Phase 2 detox, contributing sulfur and indole-3-carbonoles, which promote the encapsulation and excretion of toxins. Oftentimes these vegetables, such as cauliflower, Brussels sprouts, and cabbage, have an unappealing bitter taste or odor from their natural sulfur; however the champagne vinegar, fresh herbs, and dates balance out the sulfurous effects to produce a crunchy, salty, fat-focused salad with bright flavors that even my toddler loves.

Makes: 6 (¾-cup) servings | **Prep time:** 15 minutes | **Cook time:** 30 to 35 minutes

1 head cauliflower, stemmed, cored, and chopped into 2- to 3-inch pieces (about 5 to 6 cups loosely packed)

2 tablespoons avocado oil

5 tablespoons olive oil, divided

1 teaspoon salt, divided

3 tablespoons champagne vinegar

¼ teaspoon freshly ground black pepper

3 tablespoons torn or roughly chopped basil (about 10 leaves)

2 tablespoons chopped flat Italian parsley

1 pitted date, finely chopped

¼ cup pine nuts

1. Preheat the oven to 375°F.

2. Place the cauliflower on a baking sheet, drizzle it with the avocado oil and 1 tablespoon of olive oil, and mix until all pieces are glistening. Then sprinkle with ½ teaspoon of salt.

3. Place in the oven for 18 to 20 minutes, then shake pan and flip the cauliflower pieces to get a nice char on both sides. Bake for another 10 to 15 minutes, until it reaches the desired crunchiness. Transfer to a medium bowl and set aside.

4. In a small bowl, whisk the vinegar, remaining olive oil, pepper, and the remaining ½ teaspoon of salt to combine.

5. Pour the olive oil-vinegar mixture over the baked cauliflower, tossing to coat.

6. Sprinkle with the herbs, date, and pine nuts, tossing to combine. Serve at room temperature.

Nutrition facts per serving

Calories: 179 | **Carbohydrates:** 10g | **Fiber:** 4g | **Protein:** 3g | **Fat:** 15g

Roasted Mediterranean Vegetables (nf) (ef)

FOOD AS MEDICINE Often when eating a low-carb, high-fat diet, saturated fat is the star of the show. But monounsaturated fats, such as oleic acid found in olives and avocado, should remain a focus, as it supports hormone balance and brain health and reduces inflammation in the body.

Makes: 6 (⅔-cup) servings | Prep time: 10 to 15 minutes | Cook time: 25 to 30 minutes

4 tablespoons olive oil

½ teaspoon salt

¼ teaspoon freshly ground black pepper

2 tablespoons capers

2 tablespoons lemon juice

⅓ cup chopped Italian parsley (optional)

½ red onion, thinly sliced

1 red or orange bell pepper, sliced

2 zucchinis, chopped into 1- to 2-inch pieces

½ teaspoon coarse salt

1. Preheat the oven to 400°F.

2. In a small bowl, whisk the olive oil, salt, pepper, capers, lemon juice, and half of the parsley.

3. Spread the vegetables on a baking sheet and toss with the olive oil mixture to coat, then evenly spread out again and sprinkle with coarse salt.

4. Roast for 25 to 30 minutes, checking at 22 minutes and shaking the pan to prevent burning.

5. Top with remaining Italian parsley before serving.

Nutrition facts per serving

Calories: 122 | Carbohydrates: 9g | Fiber: 3g | Protein: 2g | Fat: 9g

Garlicky Lemon Green Beans (ef)

FOOD AS MEDICINE Green beans are a rich source of phytocompounds, including carotenoids, antioxidants, vitamins, and minerals. I classify green beans as a non-starchy vegetable in my exchange list, but they are technically legumes, though with considerably fewer lectins and phytates than your typical legumes, like black beans. And because portions tend to be smaller, green beans are tolerable in most health-supporting plans while lowering the risk of gut-damaging effects. Blanching and adding acid along with the anti-inflammatory fat from olive oil also enhances nutrient density and reduces anti-nutrients. Green beans are high in folic acid, fiber, and B vitamins; they work to protect vessel health and support bone health with vitamin K, manganese, and silica. Adding green beans into your diet may favorably impact anxiety and stress as they promote healthy levels of serotonin and dopamine with folate, vitamin B6, and vitamin C.

Makes: 4 servings | **Prep time:** 10 to 15 minutes

zest and juice of 1 lemon

2 cloves garlic, finely chopped

2 teaspoons chopped fresh oregano

½ teaspoon salt

¼ teaspoon freshly ground black pepper

¼ cup olive oil

3 cups blanched green beans

1 tablespoon torn flat Italian parsley leaves, to serve

½ teaspoon coarse salt, to serve

⅓ cup dry-roasted chopped pecans, to serve

1. In a medium bowl, mix the lemon zest, lemon juice, garlic, oregano, salt, and pepper.

2. Slowly pour in olive oil while whisking. Continue to whisk for about 30 seconds to incorporate the acid into the fat.

3. Toss the green beans in the dressing and top with parsley, coarse salt, and pecans.

4. Serve chilled or at room temperature.

Nutrition facts per serving

Calories: 216 | Carbohydrates: 10g | Fiber: 4g | Protein: 2g | Fat: 20g

Blanching 101

Blanching is the process of cooking vegetables in boiling water or steaming for a short period of time (2 to 3 minutes). The cooking process is stopped by submerging the cooked vegetables in an ice bath or running under cold water. This produces a nice crisp texture with even cooking throughout.

Crispy Broccoli (nf) (ef)

FOOD AS MEDICINE Broccoli is a potent detoxifier and hormone regulator with indole-3-carbinol compounds, including sulforaphane to support Phase 2 detoxification and reduce estrogen dominance. When the body is able to release toxins, it has less inflammatory reactivity, resulting in more energy for focus on regulation of parasympathetic (rest-digest-metabolize-reproduce) mode. Broccoli is also a great source of folate and chromium to support neurotransmitter production and blood sugar metabolism. This recipe emulates my favorite Asian flavor profiles with clean anti-inflammatory ingredients—totally guilt-free comfort food!

Makes: 6 (⅔-cup) servings | **Prep time:** 10 to 15 minutes | **Cook time:** 25 to 35 minutes

4 cups chopped broccoli florets

2 tablespoons avocado oil

½ teaspoon salt

1 teaspoon fish sauce

1 tablespoon coconut aminos

¼ teaspoon garlic powder

¼ cup cilantro leaves, to serve

1 tablespoon sesame seeds, to serve

1. Preheat the oven to 400°F.

2. Arrange the broccoli on a baking sheet and drizzle with the avocado oil, tossing and massaging broccoli in oil until all pieces are glistening, then sprinkle with salt.

3. Bake on the lower rack for 15 minutes, then pull out of oven to shake and toss.

4. Return the pan to the oven and cook for another 10 to 15 minutes until crispy and lightly browned around the edges.

5. In a large bowl, mix together the fish sauce, coconut aminos, and garlic powder. Add the roasted broccoli and toss to coat evenly.

6. Top with cilantro and sesame seeds prior to serving.

Nutrition facts per serving

Calories: 105 | **Carbohydrates:** 14g | **Fiber:** 4g | **Protein:** 3g | **Fat:** 5g

Chapter 7

Entrees

Herb-Crusted Pork Tenderloin (nf) (ef)

FOOD AS MEDICINE Pork is an excellent source of B vitamins; if pasture-raised, it will be free of added toxins and a rich source of anti-inflammatory omega-3 fatty acids as well as conjugated linoleic acids (CLAs). Although turkey is a better-known source of tryptophan, pork too is rich with the amino acid, which is a building block of serotonin. This recipe is a great quick weekday option with very little prep and fuss (and makes great leftovers in a salad, lettuce wrap, or stir fry).

Makes: 4 (5-ounce) servings | **Prep time:** 5 minutes | **Cook time:** 20 to 25 minutes

1 to 1½ pounds pork tenderloin

1 tablespoon ground cumin

1 tablespoon dried oregano

1 tablespoon fine garlic granules

½ tablespoon smoked paprika

1 tablespoon sea salt

1 tablespoon freshly ground black pepper

1. Preheat the grill to medium or around 425°F. Pull pork tenderloin out of the refrigerator and leave on the counter while you mix the seasonings.

2. Combine the cumin, oregano, garlic, paprika, sea salt, and pepper in a small bowl.

3. Using your hands, rub the seasoning mixture on the pork tenderloin, coating completely.

4. Place the seasoned tenderloin on the grill for 20 minutes, flipping it halfway through. When the pork reaches an internal temperature between 145 and 155°F, remove it from the grill.

5. Allow the meat to sit for 8 to 10 minutes before slicing and serving.

Nutrition facts per serving

Calories: 165 | Carbohydrates: 4g | Fiber: 1g | Protein: 29g | Fat: 4g

Kimchi Burger

(nf) (ef)

FOOD AS MEDICINE Cultured vegetables contain lactic acid cultures that set up camp in your gut. Not only does kimchi function as a probiotic, the cabbage has detoxifying properties. The burger patty has a lot of umami going on with the caramelized onion, fish sauce, and salty goodness, and provides mood boosters such as zinc, vitamin B12, and vitamin B6.

Makes: 4 burgers | **Prep time:** 10 to 15 minutes | **Cook time:** 10 to 15 minutes

1 pound 85/15 grass-fed ground beef

1 teaspoon fish sauce

1 teaspoon coconut aminos

1 teaspoon hot pepper sesame oil

¼ cup chopped caramelized onion

¼ teaspoon garlic powder

¼ teaspoon freshly ground black pepper

1 avocado

1 cup kimchi

4 fried eggs (optional)

1. In a medium bowl, place the ground beef, fish sauce, coconut aminos, sesame oil, onion, garlic powder, and black pepper, and mix until blended. Form into four patties.

2. Heat a 10-inch or larger cast-iron skillet to medium-high heat. Place patties on the hot pan and cook for 4 minutes.

the anti-anxiety diet cookbook

3. Flip the patties and cook for 4 to 5 minutes more to desired doneness; 8 minutes total will provide a nice medium.

4. Allow patties to rest for about 5 minutes before serving.

5. Place each patty on a plate and top with ¼ cup kimchi, ¼ sliced avocado, and a fried egg, if using.

Nutrition facts per burger (not including egg)

Calories: 318 | Carbohydrates: 6g | Fiber: 3g | Protein: 22g | Fat: 22g

Greek Meatballs with Fresh Herbs

FOOD AS MEDICINE   A family favorite in my household, meatballs are a great sheet pan dish that can be roasted along with another sheet of veggies for a quick weeknight dinner. Using the food processor to mix up these meatballs makes it even easier and mess free! Fresh herbs add a boost of antioxidants and anti-inflammatory compounds to the dish while offsetting the gaminess lamb sometimes has. Mineral-rich, grass-fed lamb provides a nice amount of zinc, iron, and bioavailable protein that may be easier to digest than beef. It can reduce food sensitivity as lamb is not as mass produced as beef.

Makes: 6 (3-meatball) servings | **Prep time:** 15 minutes | **Cook time:** 20 to 25 minutes

¼ packed cup mint leaves

½ cup chopped red onion

3 cloves garlic, smashed

2 teaspoons fresh thyme leaves

¼ packed cup fresh oregano leaves

2 teaspoons cumin

1 teaspoon salt

1 pound ground grass-fed lamb

1 pound 85/15 grass-fed ground beef

2 tablespoons almond flour

1 egg, whisked

1 tablespoon olive oil

1. Preheat the oven to 400°F. Line a baking sheet with unbleached parchment paper.

2. Combine the mint, onion, garlic, thyme, oregano, cumin, and salt in a food processor with an "s" blade. Pulse on high until well blended.

3. Add the lamb and beef, pulsing to incorporate the herb mixture, about 1 minute.

4. Once combined, add the almond flour, egg, and olive oil and continue to pulse until incorporated, about 1 minute.

5. Form the meat mixture into 18 large meatballs (about 2 heaping tablespoons) each.

6. Transfer the meatballs to the lined baking sheet and bake for 22 to 25 minutes, checking at 20 minutes. Meatballs should cook to an internal temperature of 165°F.

7. Allow the meatballs to rest for 4 to 5 minutes before serving.

8. Serve with Antipasto Salad (page 58) or Roasted Mediterranean Vegetables (page 78).

Nutrition facts per serving

Calories: 341 | Carbohydrates: 4g | Fiber: 1g | Protein: 32g | Fat: 22g

Simple Sneaky Bolognese with Greens (ef)

FOOD AS MEDICINE   Organs are among the most nutrient-dense sources of B vitamins, minerals, vitamin A, and neurological supporters such as vitamin B12, CoQ10, and choline. Pasture-raised and grass-fed sources contain lower toxicity and more nutrient density and ensure glands are not stressed or force fed, which can create an unfavorable fatty profile. This bolognese sauce is one of my go-to weeknight dinners; it comes together in about 30 minutes.

Makes: 6 servings | **Prep time:** 10 to 15 minutes | **Cook time:** 20 to 25 minutes

2 tablespoons olive oil

1 yellow onion, diced

2 tablespoons fresh chopped thyme

1 bunch basil leaves, chopped

1 teaspoon sea salt

1 teaspoon freshly ground black pepper

1 pound 85/15 grass-fed ground beef

½ pound grass-fed ground beef organs (heart and liver are best, may add kidney if desired)

1 (15-ounce) jar marinara sauce, such as Rao's (ensure olive oil is the only listed fat, no fillers, only whole-food ingredients)

4 tablespoons tomato paste

⅛ cup almond milk

2 cups finely chopped lacinato kale

1. Heat a 12-inch cast-iron skillet over medium heat. Add the olive oil and onion. Sauté, stirring occasionally, until onion begins to brown. Add the thyme, basil, salt, and pepper, then stir for 1 to 2 minutes.

2. In a medium bowl, mix the ground beef and ground organs, then add them to the pan, breaking them up with the back of a wooden spoon. Cook, stirring occasionally, until browned, about 5 minutes. Add the marinara sauce and simmer until the flavors are well combined, 10 to 15 minutes.

3. While the sauce and meat are simmering, combine the tomato paste and almond milk in a small bowl. Pour half of the tomato paste mixture into the beef and stir to incorporate.

4. Add the finely chopped kale in the last 2 to 3 minutes of cooking. Once the kale is wilted, stir in the remaining tomato paste mixture and remove from heat. Serve over zoodles or roasted vegetables and garnish with fresh herbs.

Note on the Meat Blend

I like to use a pound of "mountain lion blend" from my farmer's market, which is ¼ pound heart, ¼ pound liver, and ½ pound 85/15 ground beef. To cut the gamey flavor, I mix the premade blend with another ½ pound grass-fed ground beef.

Nutrition facts per serving

Calories: 461 | Carbohydrates: 10g | Fiber: 3g | Protein: 21g | Fat: 37g

Chicken Thighs with Braised Greens (nf) (ef)

FOOD AS MEDICINE This recipe's dark meat contains a wealth of nutrients and helps balance amino acids that can get thrown off when you eat too much lean meat. Dark meat delivers more anti-anxiety–supporting zinc and selenium and is also abundant in taurine, which supports GABA production for relaxation. The nourishing chicken thighs pair with leafy greens and antioxidant-rich seasonings to enhance neurotransmitter balance and provide methylation support.

Makes: 8 servings | **Prep time:** 10 to 15 minutes | **Cook time:** 30 to 40 minutes

2 pounds chicken thighs

1 teaspoon sea salt, plus more to taste

1 teaspoon freshly ground black pepper

2 tablespoons ghee, divided

5 tablespoons grainy mustard

1 yellow onion, diced

5 cloves garlic, chopped

1 tablespoon ground turmeric

1 tablespoon cardamom seeds

1 bunch collard greens, chiffonade into strips

¾ cup full-fat coconut milk

½ cup chicken bone broth

¼ cup chopped cilantro leaves

1. Preheat the oven to 400°F.

2. Season the chicken thighs with the sea salt and black pepper.

3. Heat a cast-iron skillet to medium-high heat and add 1 tablespoon of ghee. When melted, add the thighs bone down, skin up, to the pan and allow to brown slightly for about 4 to 5 minutes before flipping to brown on the other side for another 4 to 5 minutes. Remove from the heat and set on a plate.

4. Brush the grainy mustard over the chicken thighs.

5. Reheat the skillet to medium heat and add the remaining ghee. Once the ghee melts, add the onion and stir to coat with ghee. Sprinkle with sea salt.

6. After 3 to 4 minutes, add chopped garlic and stir to combine. Sauté until the onion is softened, 2 to 3 minutes, then add the turmeric and cardamom seeds.

7. Allow flavors to combine for a minute or so, then add the chopped greens, coconut milk, and bone broth, stirring to combine.

8. Place the chicken thighs bone down, skin up, on top of the greens and liquid, and bake for 20 minutes.

9. Remove from the oven and allow the pan to rest for about 5 minutes. Top with chopped cilantro and serve.

Nutrition facts per serving

Calories: 227 | Carbohydrates: 2g | Fiber: 1g | Protein: 24g | Fat: 13g

Crispy Rosemary Chicken with Roasted Brussels Sprouts and Leeks

(nf) (ef)

FOOD AS MEDICINE Whole real foods include both plant and animal products. Move away from boneless, skinless meats and focus on whole forms where you can imagine it growing. Cooking with bone-in, skin-on chicken provides more glycine, proline, and collagen for relaxation and improved sleep, plus it balances out amino acids. This skillet recipe uses drippings to make an incredible white wine–coconut–herb gravy that is thickened with gelatin to further boost gut lining and digestive health. The prebiotic fibers in Brussels sprouts and leeks also fuel your microbiome!

Makes: 6 (8-ounce) servings | **Prep time:** 20 to 25 minutes | **Cook time:** 40 to 45 minutes

2 tablespoons lard

1 tablespoon sea salt, divided

2 teaspoons freshly ground black pepper, divided

2½ pounds bone-in, skin-on chicken thighs

3 cups thinly sliced Brussels sprouts

2 leeks, thinly sliced from white to light green (about ½ cup)

⅔ cup chicken bone broth, divided

3 sprigs fresh thyme leaves, chopped (about 1 tablespoon)

4 to 5 sprigs fresh rosemary, chopped, divided (about 4 tablespoons)

2 cloves garlic, peeled and chopped

¼ cup white wine (I use a dry chardonnay)

juice of ½ to 1 lemon, to taste

½ cup plus 1 tablespoon full-fat coconut milk

1 teaspoon gelatin

1. Preheat the oven to 400°F. Heat two 12-inch cast-iron skillets over medium heat and add 1 tablespoon of lard to each pan.

2. As the lard is melting, sprinkle 1 teaspoon of salt and 1 teaspoon of pepper on both sides of the chicken thighs. Place the chicken thighs skin-side up in one skillet and cook for 3 minutes. Flip and cook another 4 minutes skin-side down.

3. At the same time, add the Brussels sprouts and leeks to the second skillet, stir until coated in fat, and sprinkle with 1 teaspoon of salt. Stir every 2 minutes for about 6 minutes total. This creates a nice caramelization on the sprouts. Add ⅓ cup of broth to reduce browning of the pan and allow to reduce for 1 to 2 minutes, then top with thyme and stir to combine.

4. After the broth reduces in the Brussels sprouts skillet, add the chicken to the vegetables, placing the skinside up on top of the mixture. Top with 1 tablespoon chopped rosemary and place on the middle rack of the oven for 22 to 25 minutes.

5. While chicken thighs are baking, add the garlic to the chicken skillet and reduce the drippings over low heat, about 2 to 3 minutes, stirring constantly.

6. Add the white wine to reduce browning and simmer on low, scraping the pan occasionally, for another 3 to 5 minutes until the wine reduces to about half its volume.

7. Add 2 tablespoons of lemon juice, remaining broth, and ½ cup coconut milk, whisking to combine every minute or so for 9 to 10 minutes. Add about ¾ teaspoon salt, ¾ teaspoon pepper, and 2 tablespoons chopped rosemary to the mixture and simmer for another 3 to 4 minutes.

8. In a small bowl, mix 1 tablespoon coconut milk with 1 teaspoon gelatin. Pour the gelatin–coconut milk mixture into the sauce in the pan and whisk continuously for 1 minute.

9. Reduce heat to low and simmer for 2 minutes without disturbing. Stir once more and then turn off the heat and let sauce thicken slightly prior to serving. Season with salt, pepper, and lemon juice to taste.

10. Once chicken thighs reach an internal temperature of 165°F, around 25 minutes, remove pan from oven and allow to rest 2 to 3 minutes.

11. Pour the pan sauce on top of the chicken thighs, top with remaining 1 tablespoon rosemary, and serve.

Nutrition facts per serving

Calories: 610 | Carbohydrates: 10g | Fiber: 2g | Protein: 52g | Fat: 41g

Macadamia Coconut—Crusted Halibut

FOOD AS MEDICINE   This nut crust with threads of shredded coconut transports me back to Hawaii and channels mellow island vibes. You get your omega-3, iodine, and selenium from halibut, while the warming turmeric provides a bright color, antioxidant boost, and anti-inflammatory support. Recipes for crispy-roasted fish often call for off-limits, gluten-based panko, but I love to substitute pork rinds, which are gluten-free and provide glycine to support neuromuscular relaxation and connective tissue health. The coconut-macadamia coating also works well on chicken tenders, fish, and incorporated into ground meat.

Makes: 4 servings | Prep time: 10 to 15 minutes | Cook time: 10 to 15 minutes

½ cup macadamia nuts

1 cup pork rinds

½ teaspoon smoked paprika

1 teaspoon ground turmeric

½ teaspoon salt

¼ teaspoon freshly ground black pepper

½ cup unsweetened medium-size coconut flakes

1 egg

1 pound halibut, sliced into four 2 x 3-inch strips

3 tablespoons avocado oil

1. In a food processor with an "s" blade, pulse the macadamia nuts to a fine ground texture, about 1 minute. Make sure you pulse rather than blend or you may end up with nut butter rather than nut flour.

2. Add the pork rinds and pulse to a fine ground texture, about 30 seconds, then add paprika, turmeric, salt, and pepper, pulsing to mix.

3. Add the coconut flakes and pulse to break up, keeping the flakes on the larger side for a nice texture. Transfer the mixture to a flat plate or shallow pan.

4. Whisk the egg in a small bowl. Dip a piece of fish into the egg, let the excess drip off, then dredge in the macadamia-coconut mixture to coat. Continue until all pieces are done.

5. Add avocado oil to a 12-inch cast-iron pan and heat over medium-high heat. Once hot, add the coated fish strips skin-side down and let cook for 5 minutes.

6. Flip the pieces, then cook for another 2 to 3 minutes. Then flip once more so the skin side is down again and transfer to a plate to cool for 2 to 3 minutes before serving.

Nutrition facts per serving

Calories: 430 | Carbohydrates: 4g | Fiber: 3g | Protein: 32g | Fat: 31g

Broiled Lobster with Avocado Hollandaise

(nf) (ef)

FOOD AS MEDICINE   Lobster is an indulgence, but it doesn't have to be unapproachable. Pair the luxurious meat with avocado hollandaise for a great hormone balancer. Lobster is a lean protein that is rich in vitamin B12, zinc, and selenium, which aid in mood stability, stress tolerance, and metabolic function. Broiling with a mixture of high and medium heats maintains a great texture and the naturally sweet meat. You won't miss melted butter—the dairy-free creamy avocado hollandaise maintains satiety with healthy fats and gives a punch of flavor while providing detox support. I like to serve this rich indulgence over roasted asparagus or plated next to a light Farmer's Market Salad (page 55).

Makes: 2 servings | Prep time: 5 to 10 minutes | Cook time: 10 to 15 minutes

2 (5- to 7-ounce) lobster tails

2 tablespoons avocado oil

2 tablespoons olive oil

1 teaspoon chopped fresh thyme

½ teaspoon paprika

¼ teaspoon salt

pinch of white pepper

⅔ cup Avocado Hollandaise (page 139)

1. Using a knife or kitchen shears, cut up the center of the lobster tail on the belly side and apply pressure to the sides to open the tail, exposing more lobster meat and supporting the tail to stay balanced on the backside. Place on a sheet pan.

2. Position oven rack within 6 inches of broil flame and heat broiler to medium.

3. In a small bowl, mix the avocado oil, olive oil, thyme, paprika, salt, and white pepper. Pour the oil mixture over the lobster.

4. Broil the lobster for 8 minutes. Remove from the oven, spoon some of the drippings over the lobster meat, and place back under the broiler for an additional 2 to 4 minutes. You will know the lobster is done when the flesh changes from translucent to opaque white.

5. When cooked, pull the meat gently out of the tail and serve with a generous drizzle of Avocado Hollandaise.

Nutrition facts per serving

Calories: 489 | Carbohydrates: 2g | Fiber: 2g | Protein: 33g | Fat: 39g

Crispy Fish Tacos in Cabbage Cups

FOOD AS MEDICINE   Omega-3s favorably influence mood in depression and anxiety, plus they boost metabolism and reduce inflammation. Aim to get in wild-caught fish three times per week. With this recipe you will not have to try too hard. The almond flour coating provides the comfort of a breaded texture without the gluten or corn, and the slaw provides detoxifying indole-3-carbinol to support your body's detoxification processes.

Makes: 6 servings | **Prep time:** 20 minutes | **Cook time:** 8 to 10 minutes

Crispy Fish

1 large or 2 small eggs

1 cup almond flour

pinch of cayenne pepper (optional)

1 tablespoon chili powder

½ teaspoon freshly ground black pepper

¾ teaspoon salt

½ cup avocado oil, divided

1 pound wild-caught fish, cut into 1- to 2-inch cubes (mahi mahi, black drum, and snapper work great)

Toppings

12 to 14 cabbage leaves, wide or dense stems removed

3 cups Hemp Jalapeño Cabbage Slaw (page 54)

½ cup chopped cilantro

½ cup broccoli sprouts

2 avocados, thinly sliced

⅓ cup pickled onions

1. Whisk the egg in a small bowl. In a medium bowl, combine the almond flour, cayenne pepper, chili powder, black pepper, and salt.

2. Heat a cast-iron or stainless-steel pan over medium-high heat and add half the avocado oil.

3. As oil is heating, dredge the fish pieces in the egg, then coat them in the almond flour seasoning mixture.

4. Place fish in the hot pan and cook for 2 to 3 minutes on medium heat, then flip once and cook an additional 2 to 3 minutes.

5. Set cooked fish aside and repeat with remaining oil and coated fish pieces.

6. To serve, take cabbage leaves and smash any remaining stems with a rolling pin, rocking over to break dense plant walls (if very dense, consider steaming). Layer in dressed Hemp Jalepeño Cabbage Slaw topped with 2 to 3 pieces of fish, more slaw and desired toppings.

Nutrition facts per serving

Calories: 420 | Carbohydrates: 8g | Fiber: 3g | Protein: 15g | Fat: 38g

Garlicky Pesto Shrimp on Spaghetti Squash

(ef)

FOOD AS MEDICINE When teaching clients to maintain a sustainable approach to a low-carb lifestyle, I always say channel savory. So go for bright herbs, creamy fats, and pungent flavor that keep you satisfied while creating a vehicle for nutrient density. Herby sauces provide antioxidants and antimicrobial compounds that can reduce inflammation and support healthy gut bacteria balance. Shrimp are rich in anti-inflammatory omega-3s and thyroid-boosting selenium. Wild-caught shrimp in particular have astaxanthin, a unique antioxidant for heart health, skin protection, and a defense against cellular damage.

Makes: 4 servings | Prep time: 10 to 15 minutes, plus 55 to 60 minutes to cook spaghetti squash | Cook time: 15 minutes

2 tablespoons olive oil

1 pound wild-caught shrimp, peeled and deveined

1 teaspoon salt, divided

½ teaspoon white pepper

¼ teaspoon red pepper flakes

2 cloves garlic, smashed and chopped

1 cup fresh basil leaves

2 tablespoons fresh parsley

juice of 1 lemon

¼ cup pine nuts

2 tablespoons olive oil

⅓ cup chicken bone broth

3 cups spaghetti squash, cooked and shredded

fresh herbs, to serve

1. Heat a large skillet over medium-high heat, then add olive oil and reduce heat to medium.

2. Add the shrimp and sprinkle with ½ teaspoon salt, pepper, and pepper flakes. Stir to coat in oil until glistening, then allow to cook for 4 to 6 minutes, stirring once halfway through. Shrimp is done when it's pink and no longer translucent. Transfer to a plate.

3. To make the pesto, combine the garlic, basil, parsley, remaining salt, lemon, and pine nuts in a food processor with an "s" blade and pulse. Stop to the scrape sides with a spatula as needed. When well combined into a smooth texture, about 3 minutes, drizzle in olive oil while motor is running to create an emulsified sauce.

4. Reheat pan to medium heat and deglaze with the chicken bone broth, then add 3 cups of spaghetti squash and the pesto.

5. Reduce heat to low and stir to combine flavors, simmering on low for another 2 to 3 minutes. Add shrimp back in and simmer for 1 minute.

6. Serve into four bowls and top with fresh herbs.

Nutrition facts per serving

Calories: 463 | Carbohydrates: 16g | Fiber: 4g | Protein: 31g | Fat: 31g

Chapter 8

Kids

Children are generally less metabolically handicapped (insulin resistance, toxicity, and organ damage come with the aging process and lifestyle) and more metabolically active...do they ever sit still?! This means children are likely producing ketones for favorable effects on mood and cognitive function, with less restriction on consumption of total carbs.

That said, to maintain consistency and ensure this whole cookbook applies to all readers, I kept serving sizes at adult portions. If cooking for your child, simply adjust portions based on the child's size, growth demands, and appetite. Also, for consistency and flexibility, I ensured all these recipes could fit within Phase 1 restrictions, as some children following the anti-anxiety diet for neurological or genetic metabolic conditions still need to keep total carbs at around 30 grams per day. If your child does not have these conditions, you can add starches and fruits as desired throughout the day, always pairing these carb additions with protein or fat to maintain low-glycemic balance.

When dining out, it can be difficult to turn down the crayons and kids' menu, but the options on the children's menu often are lower-quality proteins at insignificant portions, higher in refined carbohydrates and gluten, as well as industrialized oils and additives, binders, fillers, and chemicals. Overall, kids' meals at restaurants and many people's homes are low in nourishment and encourage over-consumption of carbohydrates. Many "health" foods sold to children are carbs veiled in a vegetable powder (can we say veggie straws, cereal bars, puffs?).

I am a big fan of promoting toddlers and children to eat similar dishes to those of their parents, so I had a hard time making this chapter just for kids. It is definitely applicable to all ages and provides complexity of flavors and nutrients from whole foods to nourish children for optimal cognitive and immune function, growth, and development. I worked to develop recipes that would function as transitional tools to expand your child's palate with familiar types of dishes while supporting other sections of the book.

Turkey Macadamia Nuggets with Liver (ef)

FOOD AS MEDICINE Organs are nature's superfood, rich in CoQ10, zinc, bioavailable B vitamins, and choline. Eating snout to tail encourages consumption of bone broth, skin, and organs to provide nutrient density and balance with an abundance of amino acids proline, glycine, and glutamine, which support connective tissue growth and repair as well as reduced inflammation. Unfortunately, most people consume only muscle cuts of meat, and organs are often shunned for their gamey or metallic flavor. This recipe is a gentle reintroduction to liver, with a nice texture and potent flavors from fresh herbs and lemon juice, which provides a boost of vitamin C. If you want to further hide the flavor, top your patty with avocado or aioli of choice.

Makes: 20 servings | **Prep time:** 10 to 15 minutes | **Cook time:** 25 to 30 minutes

2 pounds dark turkey meat

½ pound chicken liver, rinsed well with cold water and patted dry

1½ teaspoons salt, divided

½ teaspoon freshly ground black pepper

2 cups macadamia nuts

3 leaves collard greens, stemmed and chopped

1 cup chopped Italian parsley leaves

2 tablespoons fresh oregano leaves

¼ cup fresh basil leaves

juice and zest of 1 lemon

1 teaspoon paprika

½ teaspoon garlic powder

2 tablespoons mustard

¼ cup avocado oil

1. Preheat the oven to 350°F and line two baking sheets with parchment paper.

2. Using a food processor with an "s" blade, blend the turkey meat and liver with ½ teaspoon salt and ½ teaspoon pepper.

3. Transfer the meat to a bowl and in a clean, dry food processor, blend the macadamia nuts to make a fine nut flour.

4. Add the chopped greens, parsley, oregano, basil, lemon zest, and lemon juice, and pulse to combine without overmixing.

5. Reincorporate the meat and pulse 6 to 8 times to incorporate with the nut and greens mixture.

6. Add the remaining salt and paprika, garlic powder, and mustard, pulsing to combine or running for short spurts.

7. As the motor is going, pour in the avocado oil, then stop the machine and scoop ¼-cup patties onto a baking sheet lined with parchment paper.

8. Bake at 350°F for 25 to 30 minutes or until crispy and brown, checking at 22 minutes for doneness and using a spatula to flip the patties for the remaining cook time.

9. Allow to rest for 3 to 5 minutes before serving.

Nutrition facts per 1½ servings

Calories: 266 | Carbohydrates: 6g | Fiber: 3g | Protein: 13g | Fat: 24g

Bacon Broccoli Egg Bites (nf)

FOOD AS MEDICINE   Egg bites are a great grab-and-go option, delivering fat, protein, and veggies while keeping the kitchen clean on a chaotic weekday morning. All my egg bites, including Prosciutto Egg Cups and Caramelized Onion, Turkey, and Kale Egg Muffins, are included in *The Anti-Anxiety Diet*, but this recipe is my daughter Stella's favorite and a great way to get cruciferous veggies into kids. The caramelized onions are key for providing both moisture and flavor while delivering quercetin and other sulfur antioxidants found in alliums (onion family) to promote detoxification. Bacon and eggs are powerhouses of choline, emphasized in the Rebalance your Neurotransmitters chapter for promoting the conduction of neurotransmitter signals.

Makes: 12 egg bites | Prep time: 15 to 20 minutes | Cook time: 50 to 60 minutes

1 pound bacon

1 large broccoli crown, chopped (2 cups florets)

1 tablespoon avocado oil

1 teaspoon salt, divided

12 eggs

1 teaspoon paprika

½ teaspoon fine ground white pepper

3 tablespoons chopped fresh thyme leaves

⅛ teaspoon baking soda

1 cup Caramelized Onions (page 138)

1. Preheat the oven to 400°F. Grease a muffin pan with avocado spray or line with parchment muffin cups.

2. On a baking sheet, lay out the bacon on parchment paper and bake for 10 to 12 minutes in middle rack, checking at 10-minute mark so as not to overcook.

3. On a separate baking sheet, drizzle the chopped broccoli with avocado oil. Toss until all of the pieces are glistening, then sprinkle with ½ teaspoon salt.

4. Place the baking sheet with the broccoli in heated oven on the lower rack, under the bacon, for 15 minutes, overlapping cook time slightly with bacon. Pull out of the oven, shake and toss, then roast for another 5 to 8 minutes.

5. In a medium bowl, whisk the eggs. Once combined, season with paprika, remaining salt, white pepper, fresh thyme, and baking soda.

6. Once the broccoli is pulled from the oven, reduce the heat to 350°F. After 2 to 3 minutes, remove and chop the bacon. Add the bacon to the freshly whisked egg mixture along with the roasted broccoli and Caramelized Onion, stirring to combine.

7. Using a measuring cup or ladle, scoop ½-cup portions into each muffin tin.

8. Place the tray in the oven and bake for 22 to 28 minutes, checking for doneness at the 20-minute mark. Egg bites will rise and when done, a toothpick inserted in the middle will come out clean and not wet.

9. Allow to sit at room temperature 3 to 5 minutes prior to serving. Store leftovers in an airtight container in the fridge for up to 5 days.

Nutrition facts per egg bite

Calories: 267 | Carbohydrates: 3g | Fiber: 1g | Protein: 20g | Fat: 20g

Shredded Rotisserie Chicken Tacos (nf) (ef)

FOOD AS MEDICINE   We follow the taco Tuesday weekly meal plan in our household and will do anything from flaky white fish to grass-fed ground beef tacos. These are also a common return-from-out-of-town hack as I start a pot of bone broth to reuse the carcass of a rotisserie chicken. Often rotisseries can get dried out, so using bone broth and seasonings is a great way to rehydrate and flavor the pulled meat while also boosting nutrient density. Cumin goes great in tacos and as a warming topping on most proteins.

Makes: 6 servings | **Prep time:** 5 to 10 minutes | **Cook time:** 25 to 30 minutes

1 tablespoon olive oil

2 tablespoons avocado oil

1 small red onion, peeled and diced (about ¾ cup)

1 clove garlic, peeled, smashed, and chopped

1 tablespoon chili powder

2 teaspoons ground cumin

1 teaspoon salt

1 red pepper, cored and diced (about 1 to 1½ cups)

1 orange pepper, cored and diced (about 1 to 1½ cups)

2 to 3 cups chicken bone broth

3 to 4 cups shredded chicken

1. Heat a 12-inch cast-iron skillet over medium-high heat. Add the olive oil and avocado oil, tilting the skillet to coat.

2. When the skillet is hot and the oil is distributed, add the onion, stirring to coat, then leave undisturbed for 2 to 3 minutes.

3. Add the garlic, chili powder, cumin, and salt, and stir to combine. Continue to sauté for another 4 to 5 minutes.

4. Add the bell peppers and stir to coat with seasonings. After 30 seconds, add 1 cup of bone broth and stir to deglaze pan.

5. Continue to sauté the vegetables and soften the bell peppers, adding broth in ½-cup increments every 4 to 5 minutes.

6. Once the peppers are softened, about 10 to 12 minutes, add the shredded chicken with ½ cup broth, and stir once more to combine all flavors.

7. Sauté for an additional 3 to 5 minutes, adding ½ cup of broth at the end and cooking for another 2 to 3 minutes to absorb the liquid.

Serving ideas

Toddlers: Serve on a plate for them to eat with their fingers or in a bowl with avocado cubes to eat with a fork.

Kids: Try serving on lettuce "taco shells," lettuce leaves topped with avocado slices and optional salsa.

Adults: Add your favorite hot sauce to taste as well as fresh cilantro and pickled onions. Serve on a salad of greens or in lettuce cups (or taco shells).

Nutrition facts per serving

Calories: 317 | **Carbohydrates:** 11g | **Fiber:** 2g | **Protein:** 46g | **Fat:** 10g

Almond Flour Chicken Tenders

FOOD AS MEDICINE This recipe is a family favorite and pleasing to palates of all ages! I like to make it in rotation with wings during football season and always make a double batch to have some frozen on hand to top a salad or for a mid-week survival meal. Consider serving with your favorite avocado-based mayo, mixed with mustard or truffle salt for a fancy aioli, or dipping in my MCT Oil Ketchup (page 137). These tenders have so much flavor and the textured almond flour coating keeps in the moisture so they stand alone just fine if you aren't into dipping.

Makes: 4 (2- to 3-tender) servings | Prep time: 10 to 15 minutes | Cook time: 20 to 25 minutes

1 to 2 teaspoons ghee

1 pound boneless, skinless pasture-raised chicken breasts

¾ cup almond meal

½ teaspoon garlic powder

2 teaspoons paprika

1 teaspoon sea salt

½ teaspoon white pepper

2 eggs, lightly beaten

1. Preheat the oven to 375°F and grease a baking sheet with the ghee.

2. Place the chicken breasts in a zip-top freezer bag and pound to 1-inch thickness. Slice the chicken breasts into long, 1- to 2-inch-wide strips.

3. In a shallow baking dish, mix together the almond meal, garlic powder, paprika, sea salt, and pepper.

4. Dredge each piece of chicken in egg then coat with almond spice mixture.

5. Place the chicken on the ghee-coated baking sheet in the middle of the oven and bake for 20 to 25 minutes until golden and cooked throughout, with juices running clear.

Note: I like to make a double batch and use a second baking sheet to lay out the other half of the recipe. Then I freeze the chicken fingers on the baking sheet and, once frozen, store in a freezer bag layered with parchment paper. Frozen chicken will require longer baking time of 30 to 40 minutes but will turn out great!

Nutrition facts per serving

Calories: 303 | Fat: 18g | Carbohydrates: 6g | Protein: 33g

Turkey Apple Kale Patties

(ef)

FOOD AS MEDICINE Greens are a powerful player for metabolic and mood stability. They are rich in folate, magnesium, and B vitamins while providing volume and fiber to fuel healthy gut bacteria. Greens can be tricky with children but I recommend getting them in daily! Start teaching your children about bitter flavors and introduce them to raw greens in salads and smoothies within their first 18 months, definitely by age 2. This patty has a nice balance of flavor with the natural sweetness of apple and sautéed onion and the herbaceous blend of parsley and lacinato kale. This recipe is a school lunch favorite and tastes great both hot and cold.

Makes: 6 (2-meatball or -patty) servings | Prep time: 15 to 20 minutes | Cook time: 35 to 40 minutes

2 tablespoons avocado oil, divided

1 cup chopped apple (with skin on; I used Honey Crisp)

½ cup peeled and chopped red onion

½ teaspoon plus generous pinch of salt

3 cups stemmed and chopped lacinato kale

⅓ cup flat Italian parsley leaves

½ teaspoons white pepper

1 pound ground dark turkey meat

2 tablespoons almond flour

1. Preheat the oven to 350°F and line a baking sheet with parchment paper.

2. Heat a skillet over medium-high heat and add 1 tablespoon avocado oil followed by the apple and onion.

3. Stir the apple and onion to coat in oil and allow to simmer undisturbed for 2 to 3 minutes. Turn the heat down to medium, then stir every 2 minutes or so for 8 minutes.

4. Add generous pinch of salt and the kale leaves. Stir again to coat the leaves, which will start to wilt down. Continue sautéing for 5 to 6 minutes.

5. Once the kale has cooked down, turn off heat and allow mixture to cool.

6. Once cooled, transfer the kale mixture to a food processor with an "s" blade. Add remaining ½ teaspoon salt, parsley, and white pepper, and pulse until well combined.

7. Add the turkey and pulse 10 to 15 times to mix well.

8. Add the almond flour and pulse about 5 to 6 times to incorporate.

9. Scoop ⅛-cup portions into hands and roll into patties or meatballs. Place the patties on a baking sheet.

10. Transfer the baking sheet to the oven for 20 to 25 minutes, checking for doneness at 20 minutes. Bake until lightly browned and the internal temperature reaches 165°F.

Nutrition facts per serving

Calories: 189 | Carbohydrates: 5g | Fiber: 1g | Protein: 15g | Fat: 13g

Broccoli Bacon Sweet Potato Tots

FOOD AS MEDICINE   These tots are legit. They provide an awesome crunchy mouthfeel and a nice blend of sweet and savory. They go great with a simple protein and include both a green, sulfur-containing veggie and a starch without breaking your keto bank. The sweet potato provides carotenoids, soluble fiber, and specific antioxidants that promote the growth of favorable mood-boosting probiotics bifidobacterium and lactobacillus. Another rule of thumb of mine, beyond "pair all carbs with protein or fat," (which this recipe does with bacon, coconut, and avocado oil) is "when in doubt...add bacon!" It works well for encouraging your child's intake of veggies and broccoli, which can be subbed with cauliflower, Brussels sprouts, and so much more in this recipe.

Makes: 6 (5-tot) servings | Prep time: 15 to 20 minutes | Cook time: 20 to 30 minutes

1 cup roasted sweet potato, finely chopped

3 to 5 cups water

2 cups chopped broccoli

¼ cup chopped fresh basil leaves

4 strips bacon, cooked and chopped

⅛ cup fresh Italian parsley leaves

½ teaspoon salt, divided

¼ teaspoon freshly ground black pepper

3 tablespoons finely chopped red onion

1 egg, room temperature

⅓ cup almond flour

1 tablespoon coconut flour

avocado oil spray

1. Preheat the oven to 400°F.

2. Roast a sweet potato (see instructions below) and chop it up.

3. In a medium pot fitted with a steamer basket, bring 3 to 5 cups of water to a boil.

4. Place the chopped broccoli into the steamer basket and steam for 6 to 8 minutes until the broccoli is bright green and cooked through.

5. Set the broccoli aside to cool, then chop it to a fine mince. Add the broccoli and roasted sweet potato to a large bowl.

6. Add the chopped basil, bacon, parsley, ¼ teaspoon salt, pepper, and red onion, stirring to combine.

7. In a small bowl, whisk the egg, then add it to the vegetable and herb blend. Stir well to coat.

8. In another bowl, mix the almond flour, coconut flour, and remaining salt, then sprinkle the mixture slowly into the vegetable herb blend, allowing the nut flours to thicken and distribute throughout.

9. Spray a baking sheet with the avocado oil. Using a heaping tablespoon measuring spoon, scoop and pack the broccoli mixture into rough oval tot shapes, and place them on a baking sheet.

10. Once the tots are lined up on baking sheet, spray once more with avocado oil.

11. Bake for 20 to 30 minutes, checking at 18 minutes and using a spatula to flip tots for the remaining cook time.

12. If looking dry, consider spraying with avocado oil again before placing back in the oven for 5 to 15 minutes, as needed.

13. Allow to rest for 3 to 5 minutes before serving.

Nutrition facts per serving

Calories: 125 | Carbohydrates: 10g | Fiber: 4g | Protein: 5g | Fat: 8g

Roasting Sweet Potatoes

Preheat the oven to 400°F. Cut 1 large sweet potato into ½-inch cubes (about 2½ cups). Toss with 2 tablespoons melted coconut oil and evenly distribute in a single layer on a baking sheet; do no overlap the pieces. Sprinkle with ⅔ teaspoon salt and bake in the oven's middle rack for 25 to 35 minutes, checking at 22 minutes, turning over with a spatula, and assessing whether it is cooked through to determine remaining bake time. This makes 2 cups.

Stella's Simple Wild Salmon

(nf) (ef)

FOOD AS MEDICINE Wild-caught salmon is rich in omega-3 fatty acids, including EPA for anti-inflammatory support and DHA for brain support. Both aid in mood stability and alleviating anxiety. Salmon was my daughter Stella's first protein. Following baby-led weaning at 9 months, she immediately took to it and, at age 3, still eats 4 to 6 ounces when she is offered, much more than any other protein she consumes. Grass-fed beef is a close second.

Teach your children early on to be open to pungent flavors, and work with them by adding more fat and salt until it is palatable. These things can be adjusted over time, if needed. As a source of biological protein, salmon provides vitamin D, B vitamins, selenium, and unique antioxidants such as astaxanthin to enhance brain health and reduce oxidative damage.

Makes: 4 servings | **Prep time:** 5 minutes | **Cook time:** 8 to 12 minutes

4 (5-ounce) wild thawed or fresh salmon fillets, skin on, deboned

2 tablespoons avocado oil

½ teaspoon salt

¼ teaspoon freshly ground black pepper

¼ teaspoon dried dill

½ teaspoon chopped fresh parsley, plus more to serve (optional)

lemon slices, to serve (optional)

1. Preheat the oven to 400°F. Place the salmon skin-side down on a small baking sheet lined with parchment paper.

2. Drizzle the avocado oil over the fillets, using a brush or fingertips to spread the oil over the surface.

3. Sprinkle with salt, pepper, dill, and parsley.

4. Bake in the oven for 8 to 12 minutes, checking at 8 minutes to determine if additional time is needed for a medium cook with a light red center or an internal temperature of 145°F.

5. Allow to cool for 2 to 3 minutes prior to serving. Top with lemon slices and more fresh parsley, if using.

Nutrition facts per serving

Calories: 187 | **Carbohydrates:** 0g | **Fiber:** 0g | **Protein:** 30g | **Fat:** 8g

Almond Butter Banana Pancakes

FOOD AS MEDICINE   This recipe is in weekly rotation in my home. I love making a double batch to include pancake pieces in my daughter's lunch or weekday breakfasts. I am all about a pancake that includes nut butter, eggs, and banana as main ingredients. Before you freak out about banana being high carb, check out how awesome the macros are with a serving of two pancakes likely still working even in a tight Phase 1 keto. The banana adds a perfect texture and lightness while serving as a prebiotic to feed your microbiome and providing tryptophan and B6 to boost serotonin. This recipe is a great way to start the day with grounding fats and protein, especially if paired with a side of bacon and topped with coconut cream, nut butter, or ghee.

Makes: 6 (2- to 3-pancake) servings | **Prep time:** 5 minutes | **Cook time:** 8 to 10 minutes

1 large banana, about ⅔ cup mashed

3 large eggs

½ cup almond butter

¼ teaspoon baking soda

½ teaspoon vanilla extract

pinch of salt

4 teaspoons avocado oil

1. In a blender, combine all of the ingredients except for the avocado oil. Blend on medium speed for about 1 minute.

2. Heat a skillet over medium heat and add 1 to 2 teaspoons of avocado oil, turning the pan to coat evenly.

3. Use a ⅛-cup measurer to scoop batter from blender and pour 3 to 4 pancakes into the skillet. If you don't have a ⅛-cup measurer, eyeball half of ¼ cup per scoop.

4. Cook until tiny bubbles form at the surface, about 3 minutes, then flip once with a spatula.

5. Cook on the other side for 2 to 3 minutes and plate the pancakes. Repeat with the remaining avocado oil and batter.

Nutrition facts per serving

Calories: 334 | **Carbohydrates:** 13g | **Fiber:** 5g | **Protein:** 12g | **Fat:** 27g

Which Almond Butter to Use?

Grinding your own almond butter at the grocery store works best. But if your store doesn't do this, choose an almond butter with only almonds and salt, and stir to incorporate prior to measuring. Shop all my recommended products in the Building an Anti-Anxiety Diet Pantry in the Anti-Anxiety Diet Guide at www.alimillerrd.com/anti-anxiety-diet-guide.

Cinnamon Protein Nut Butter Balls

(ef)

FOOD AS MEDICINE   These nut butter balls taste like cookie dough, yet don't have any added sugar. The natural sweetness of dates provide a rich boost of minerals and B vitamins while the healthy fats in the coconut oil and nuts support a sustained release of fuel, preventing big blood sugar spikes, which mellows out mood and energy. If whey is not tolerated, consider substituting collagen peptides to support structural function, gut health, and provide protein. To add another medicinal component, you may consider mixing in my Restore Baseline Probiotic to boost immune function and microbiome.

Makes: 20 balls | **Prep time:** 15 minutes | **Set time:** 30 to 60 minutes

1 cup raw almonds

1 cup raw pecan halves

½ teaspoon salt

1 tablespoon coconut oil

1 tablespoon almond butter

1 scoop (30 grams) grass-fed whey or 3 scoops (24 grams) collagen peptides

3 pitted dates

½ teaspoon ground cinnamon

1 tablespoon cashew butter

5 quality 15 billion CFU probiotics capsules, such as Naturally Nourished Restore Baseline Probiotic (optional)

1. In a food processor with an "s" blade, add the almonds, pecans, and salt. Mix for about 45 seconds, pulsing a couple times during, until finely ground and a small line of nut butter about ⅛ inch thick starts to form at the bottom.

2. Add the coconut oil, almond butter, and whey or collagen peptide, mixing for another 20 seconds. Add the dates and pulse 20 to 25 times to combine.

3. Finally, add the cinnamon and cashew butter. If using probiotic capsules, open capsules and sprinkle in the contents, then mix until mixture starts to form a large mass or ball. Do not overmix; once a ball starts to form in the food processor, stop. Use a half-filled tablespoon to scoop mixture into 20 portions, then use palms of hands to roll into small balls. Set in fridge to solidify for at least 30 minutes, storing for up to 2 weeks.

Note: If using recommended probiotic, each serving provides 3.75 billion CFU of probiotics.

Nutrition facts per ball

Calories: 121 | **Carbohydrates:** 5g | **Fiber:** 7g | **Fat:** 9g

Chapter 9

Indulgences

Walnut Maca Caramels (ef)

FOOD AS MEDICINE   Walnuts are a rich source of omega-3s that reduce inflammation and anxiety. Beyond omega-3s, walnuts are a great source of polyphenols, antioxidants that have disease-fighting properties. This property in the bitter skin is antimicrobial and antiparasitic, aiding in resetting the microbiome and reducing inflammation. Luckily this recipe balances out the bitterness of the skin with vanilla, salt, and dates. Another potent anti-anxiety player in this treat is maca. Maca is a Peruvian root vegetable that has adaptogenic properties. Adaptogens aid in stress response, preventing stress-induced fatigue and adrenal distress. As the adrenals are preserved, other glands in the body have the ability to shine, which means more balanced thyroid and sexual hormones too!

Makes: 12 large or 24 small balls | **Prep time:** 10 to 15 minutes

1½ cups walnuts

1 teaspoon sea salt

2 tablespoons maca powder

1 tablespoon vanilla extract

3 to 9 dates, pitted and chopped, to taste

1. In a food processor with an "s" blade, combine the walnuts and sea salt.

2. Blend until combined into a fine meal and a thin line of nut butter starts to form on the side of the container.

3. Scrape the sides of the food processor container with a spatula, and add the maca and vanilla.

4. Blend for another 15 to 20 seconds and scrape sides again, then add 3 pitted chopped dates, about 3 tablespoons.

5. Blend for another 20 to 30 seconds, scrape the sides, and taste. Adjust by adding more dates and sea salt as desired.

6. With your hands, roll the mixture into 1- to 2-tablespoon balls. Store in the fridge.

Nutrition facts per 1 large (2-tablespoon) ball

Calories: 131 calories | **Carbohydrates:** 10g | **Fiber:** 2g | **Protein:** 3g | **Fat:** 10g

Raspberry Cream Panna Cotta (nf) (ef)

FOOD AS MEDICINE This bright acidic recipe provides a beautiful rich-pink hue and is a nice play on panna cotta, using quality-sourced gelatin to balance out amino acids in the body, promote relaxation, and support gut lining repair. The adrenals get supported with this recipe with a boost of vitamin C from berries and lemon juice. They also pair nicely with gelatin as vitamin C is important in connective tissue repair. This is a great protein and fat-based evening treat when staying tight in your keto diet. As your palate resets you will not need to add any sweetener to the creamy and naturally sweet coconut.

Makes: 4 servings | **Prep time:** 5 to 10 minutes | **Set time:** 4 to 8 hours

1½ cups raspberries

1 (13.5-ounce) can full-fat coconut milk

½ lemon, juiced (about 1 tablespoon)

1 tablespoon gelatin

1. Blend all of the ingredients on high for 45 to 60 seconds, until well incorporated.

2. Allow to sit in the blender for 5 minutes to bloom the gelatin, then blend on high for 1 minute and pour the mixture into 4 glass jars or containers with lids.

3. Refrigerate for at least 4 hours to allow gelatin to set before serving.

Nutrition facts per serving

Calories: 206 | Carbohydrates: 9g | Fiber: 3g | Protein: 2g | Fat: 18g

Gelatin for Gut Restoration and Tissue Repair

Gelatin is comprised of glycine and proline, two amino acids that are abundant in organs, bones, and fibrous animal tissues but not commonly consumed in the modern American diet. These amino acids contribute to healthy skin and promote collagen formation as well as hair and nail strength. Gelatin can be therapeutic for bone and joint support, showing promising research and outcomes superior to most supplements. Its main claim to fame is the ability to line the gut and reduce inflammation caused by food allergies or inflammatory bowel disease. Gelatin has mucilaginous (aka "oopy-goopy") compounds that reline the gut, essentially serving as a face-lift for the GI tract and fuel for the gut cells! Beyond these benefits, there is some compelling research that suggests it may reduce cellulite and boost weight loss. With all these benefits, break out the gelatin (grass-fed sources only, not your standard confined animal farm sources used by Jell-O or Knox) and get in the kitchen!

Lemon Lavender CBD Balls (ef)

FOOD AS MEDICINE Along with chamomile, lavender is the most popular nervine herb, used for thousands of years to aid in anxiety, depression, convulsions, and even as a sedative. Nervines are plants that have a positive influence on the nervous system, supporting relaxation and release of tension. Along with adaptogens, nervines are among my top recommendations for aiding in stress tolerance and resilience. The addition of lavender petals to CBD oil mellows out stress response and supports restful rebound. As a dense delivery of fat, these balls are a great tonifying way to break a fast on a stressful day or end the day with your feet up, breathing in serenity for a restful evening.

Makes: 12 balls | Prep time: 10 to 15 minutes | Set time: 20 to 45 minutes

1¼ cups Brazil nuts

⅔ cup macadamia nuts

¼ cup coconut oil, melted

¼ teaspoon salt

2 teaspoons lavender, divided

1 heaping teaspoon lemon zest (from 1 lemon)

1 teaspoon vanilla extract

½ teaspoon raw unfiltered honey

2 mL CBD oil (about 70mg CBD)

1. In a food processor with an "s" blade, blend the Brazil nuts and macadamia nuts for 1 minute, until a 1-inch-thick nut butter forms at the base of the food processor.

2. Add the melted coconut oil, salt, 1 heaping teaspoon lavender, lemon zest, vanilla extract, honey, and CBD oil, and pulse to combine.

3. Blend once more on process mode for about 30 to 45 seconds until one large mass starts to form.

4. Use a silicone spatula to scrape into a bowl. Set in the freezer for 15 to 20 minutes to allow the coconut oil to harden and thicken.

5. Use a small scoop or tablespoon to scoop out 12 heaping balls on a parchment paper–lined tray or plate. Topping balls with remaining lavender and lemon zest.

6. Place the balls in the freezer to set for about 20 to 45 minutes, then transfer to an airtight glass container. Store in the freezer for up to 10 days.

7. Consume within 5 to 10 minutes of removing from the freezer as the coconut oil will melt quickly.

Nutrition facts per ball

Calories: 177 | **Carbohydrates:** 3g | **Fiber:** 2g | **Protein:** 2g | **Fat:** 18g

What Is CBD Oil?

CBD oil (cannabidiol): This non-psychoactive compound found in cannabis may be used foundationally or as a demand-based tool to promote GABA expression in the brain, which supports an inhibitory impact on stress response, reducing reactivity. The human body is hard-wired with cannabinoid receptors, which CBD can interact with to yield beneficial anti-anxiety effects. CBD has a role in supporting neurological function and regulating nervous system and stress signals as well as supporting the immune system and reducing inflammation. To learn more about CBD oil and other anti-anxiety diet supplements, download the Anti-Anxiety Diet Guide at www.alimillerrd.com/anti-anxiety-diet-guide.

Hemp Nut Bars with Chocolate (ef)

FOOD AS MEDICINE   Hemp seeds provide essential fats, including gamma-linolenic acid (GLA), which supports skin and hormonal health. GLA favorably reduces excess prolactin in the body, which, when elevated, contributes to hormone imbalance, irregular cycles, infertility, low libido, belly fat, and menopause symptoms. Hemp seeds also provide a nice boost of mood-stabilizing minerals while almonds and pecans enhance fiber content. The dark chocolate drizzle provides a nice bitter play on the bar base with polyphenols to support blood pressure and vascular health, and the bitter alkaloid theobromine, when combined with the naturally occurring caffeine in chocolate, can act as a stimulant and mood boost.

Makes: 9 (2 x 2-inch) bars | Prep time: 15 minutes | Set time: 1 hour

Base

1 cup raw almonds

1 cup raw pecan halves

¼ cup hemp seeds

½ teaspoon salt

1 tablespoon coconut oil

2 dates, pitted and torn into tiny pieces

2 tablespoons almond butter

Toppings

¼ cup 85% cacao pieces

1 tablespoon coconut oil

1 tablespoon hemp seeds

1 tablespoon freeze-dried raspberries

1. In a food processor with an "s" blade, add the almonds, pecans, hemp seeds, and salt, mixing for about 45 seconds, Pulse a couple of times during until finely ground and a ⅛-inch-thick line of nut butter starts to form at the bottom.

2. Add the coconut oil, date pieces, and almond butter. Mix until the mixture starts to gather into a large mass or ball. Do not overmix; once a ball forms, stop.

3. Line an 8 x 8-inch pan with parchment paper and press the mixture into the pan with a spatula or your fingers to cover an 8 x 6-inch area or so, setting up for 3 rows of 3, or 9 rectangles. Place in the freezer to set.

4. While the base is setting, create a double boiler by simmering water in a small pot and placing a bowl or smaller pot on top.

5. Place the chocolate pieces and coconut oil in the bowl or pot and allow to melt, stirring with a spatula.

6. Remove the base from the freezer and drizzle the chocolate on top. Sprinkle with the remaining toppings.

7. Serve immediately with warm melted chocolate on top or set in the freezer for 5 to 10 minutes to allow toppings to firm.

8. Store in an airtight container in the freezer for up to 1 week. Thaw each piece for about 5 to 8 minutes before eating. Don't thaw completely or coconut oil will melt.

Nutrition facts per bar

Calories: 253 | Carbohydrates:10g | Fiber: 4g fiber | Protein: 6g | Fat: 23g

Coconut Macaroons

FOOD AS MEDICINE   This is a simple, subtly sweet recipe that provides a nice texture and chew. Be sure to save your egg yolks for the following morning's scramble to benefit from their redeeming nutrients, such as choline. This is a great recipe for a gut cleanse, such as my Beat the Bloat 6-week protocol, as the caprylic acid aids in antimicrobial and antifungal action in the gut, while a decent hit of fiber supports bowel detoxification. As coconut is also a great source of MCT, these treats maintain a healthy state of nutritional ketosis, supporting mitochondria and energy production and making a great occasional indulgence or balanced daily snack.

Makes: 12 cookies | Prep time: 15 to 20 minutes | Cook time: 12 to 15 minutes

2 cups unsweetened shredded coconut

¼ teaspoon baking soda

¼ teaspoon salt

1 tablespoon gelatin

1 tablespoon coconut oil, melted

1 tablespoon raw unfiltered honey

1 teaspoon almond extract

3 egg whites

½ cup unsweetened large coconut flakes

3 ounces 85% cacao baking bar (I use Theo)

1. Line a baking sheet with parchment paper and preheat the oven to 325°F.

2. In a large bowl, combine the shredded coconut, baking soda, salt, and gelatin.

3. In a separate small bowl, combine the coconut oil, honey, and almond extract. Once mixed, stir into the large bowl of dried ingredients.

4. Using an electric mixer, beat the egg whites on high with a whisk for about 2 minutes until large white peaks of foam form.

5. Fold the egg white foam into the coconut mixture and, once combined, add in the coconut flakes.

6. Place the batter in heaping tablespoons on the baking sheet and bake for 12 to15 minutes until lightly browned.

7. Pull the macaroons from the oven and allow to cool.

8. While the macaroons are cooling at room temperature, heat a pot of water to a boil and place a glass or metal bowl on top to create a double boiler.

9. Break up the chocolate bar into the bowl and stir with a rubber spatula every 30 seconds or so to slowly melt the chocolate.

10. Once melted, remove the bowl from the heat and drizzle the chocolate with a spatula over the macaroons.

11. Place the chocolate-drizzled macaroons in freezer to set for 10 to 15 minutes. Serve and store leftovers in the fridge for 4 to 5 days or freezer for up to 4 weeks, if they last that long.

Nutrition facts per cookie

Calories: 144 | Carbohydrates: 8g | Fiber: 3g | Protein: 2g | Fat: 12g

Low-Carb Chocolate Chip Cookies

FOOD AS MEDICINE Creating a health-supportive dish is all about composition and real food ingredients. In this case, a chocolate chip cookie fits the bill. Healthy fats ground energy levels, support adrenals, and regulate blood sugar levels. This recipe provides a nostalgic treat without a sugar bomb causing a crash later in the day. With minimal amounts of dark chocolate, maple, and molasses, one or two cookies a couple times a week can easily fit in a ketogenic lifestyle. Keeping to real sweeteners in small amounts allows some nutritive benefit while encouraging a true reset of your relationship to sweet.

Makes: 12 cookies | **Preparation time:** 15 minutes | **Cook time:** 15 minutes

1¼ cups almond flour

½ teaspoon baking soda

¼ teaspoon salt

1 scoop collagen peptides (8 grams)

1 teaspoon gelatin

3 tablespoons almond butter

2 tablespoons coconut butter, softened

2 tablespoons coconut oil

1 tablespoon robust, dark amber maple syrup

1 tablespoon molasses

1 teaspoon vanilla extract

1 large egg, whisked

⅛ cup Pasha 100% cacao chips, or at least 85% dark chocolate chips (ensure soy-free)

1. Preheat the oven to 350°F and line a baking sheet with parchment paper.

2. In a mixer, combine the first five ingredients, and mix to combine.

3. In a separate bowl, combine the remaining ingredients (except the cacao chips). Once the wet ingredients are combined, add them to the mixer and continue to blend for 1 minute to make a dough.

4. Once a dough is formed, add the cacao chips and stir with a spoon to incorporate.

5. Scoop 12 heaping spoonfuls of batter on the baking sheet.

6. Bake for 10 to 12 minutes, checking at 10 minutes for a golden hue and slightly crisped edges. Cool for 5 minutes before serving for best texture and form.

Nutrition facts per cookie

Calories: 166 | **Carbohydrates:** 6g | **Fiber:** 2g | **Protein:** 5g | **Fat:** 13g

Chia Cherry Thumbprint Cookies (ef)

FOOD AS MEDICINE Chia seeds are packed with anti-inflammatory omega-3 fatty acids, as well as a substantial amount of fiber. They are a great addition to smoothies, breakfasts, and desserts, providing a gel-like consistency to fruit puree. Although this recipe is an indulgence, the higher fiber and healthy fats from almond flour and coconut oil help stabilize blood sugar and create a feeling of satiety, satisfying your sweet tooth for longer. This recipe supports relaxation, as the red and purple pigmentation in cherries, known as anthocyanin, helps regulate blood flow. In addition, cherries provide melatonin for improving sleep quality, resetting circadian rhythm, and reducing anxiety throughout the following day.

Makes: 12 cookies | **Prep time:** 15 to 20 minutes | **Cook time:** 10 to 12 minutes

Jam

¾ cup dried cherries (unsulphured, with no added sugar), soaked in ¼ cup warm water

1 tablespoon dark amber maple syrup

1 to 2 tablespoons filtered water, divided

3 tablespoons chia seeds

Cookies

1½ cups almond flour

¼ cup coconut flour

2 tablespoons almond butter

1 teaspoon baking soda

⅓ cup coconut oil, melted

2 tablespoons dark amber maple syrup

½ teaspoon vanilla extract

½ teaspoon almond extract

¼ teaspoon sea salt

1. Preheat the oven to 350°F. Line a baking sheet with parchment paper.

2. In a food processor with an "s" blade, combine the soaked cherries with their soaking water, maple syrup, and 1 tablespoon of water. Process until smooth, adding the rest of the water as needed. Once combined, pulse in the chia seeds. Scoop out into a small bowl and allow to sit for at least 15 minutes while you make the cookies. This allows your "jam" to gel.

3. Combine the almond flour, coconut flour, almond butter, baking soda, coconut oil, maple syrup, vanilla extract, almond extract, and sea salt in food processor with an "s" blade. Mix until a uniform dough forms into a ball.

4. Scoop out the dough one heaping tablespoon at a time and roll into smooth balls between the palms of your hands. Place on a baking sheet and use your thumb to create a well in the middle for the jam. Scoop one teaspoon of chia jam into each cookie.

5. Bake 10 to 12 minutes until the tops begin to brown. Remove from the oven and let cool at least 15 minutes before serving.

Nutrition facts per cookie

Calories: 155 | Carbohydrates: 14g | Fiber: 4g | Protein: 3g | Fat: 10g

Keto Avocado Brownies

FOOD AS MEDICINE   These dense, chewy brownies are a great example of a real-food keto recipe. Using almond flour and avocados as the foundation, they provide healthy fats and fiber to support satiety, brain health, and blood sugar balance, as well as B vitamins to boost neurotransmitter production. The jammy date paste aids in hydrating and sweetening the brownies while providing a nice rich mouthfeel. These brownies are a great way to restore micronutrient deficiency, with rich, mood-stabilizing minerals, fats, and antioxidants to promote cellular health. In my household, we add fresh-cut fruit like berries and whipped coconut milk on top for guests who need a bit more sweet, but they stand on their own just fine.

Makes: 12 (2 x 1-inch) brownies | Prep time: 30 to 45 minutes | Cook time: 20 to 25 minutes

4 dates, pitted

⅛ cup warm water

½ cup mashed avocados (about 1½ medium avocados)

1 medium egg

2 egg yolks

2 teaspoons vanilla extract

2 teaspoons almond extract

½ cup cacao powder

⅓ cup almond flour

¾ teaspoon baking soda

½ teaspoon sea salt

¼ cup melted coconut oil

¼ cup melted ghee or coconut butter

⅛ cup cashew butter

2 ounces coarsely chopped 80% cacao chocolate bar

¼ cup coarsely chopped nuts, like pecans or walnuts (optional)

1. Preheat the oven to 350°F.

2. Place the dates in a small bowl with the warm water and soak for at least 30 minutes, longer if dates are dense and dry, to soften to a squishy texture.

3. Once they are softened, pulse the dates with the soaking water using a food processor with an "s" blade until a paste forms.

4. Add the avocado and blend until combined.

5. In a medium bowl, whisk the egg with the additional 2 yolks. Add the vanilla and almond extracts, then add the egg mixture to the food processor. Wait to mix again.

6. In a separate bowl, combine the cacao powder, almond flour, baking soda, and sea salt.

7. Add the dry ingredients to the food processor with the egg mixture and avocado-date blend and blend for about 30 seconds.

8. In a small bowl, use a whisk to mix together the melted coconut oil, ghee, and cashew butter. Pour the melted mixture (make sure it is warm, not hot) into the food processor and blend all of the ingredients for about 15 seconds.

9. Spread the brownie mixture into a greased 8 × 8-inch pan.

10. Sprinkle the brownies with chocolate chunks and nuts, if using, and bake in the oven in the middle rack for about 20 minutes, checking at 18 minutes and removing them when corners pull from edges of pan and a cake tester comes out clean.

11. Allow to cool completely, then cut into 12 pieces.

12. Store for up to 1 week in an airtight glass container at room temperature or in the fridge for a denser, fudgy brownie.

Nutrition facts per brownie

Calories: 204 | Carbohydrates: 12g | Fiber: 3g | Protein: 3g | Fat: 17g

Cashew Beet "Cheese" Cake (ef)

FOOD AS MEDICINE This cheesecake is a decadent delivery of brain-boosting fat with brilliantly bright color, making a statement appropriate for a birthday treat or indulgent dessert. The use of gelatin to bind and solidify the base supports gut health. Soaking the nuts reduces anti-nutrients and gut-irritating compounds while aiding in nutrient absorption. There is no feeling of missing out when having this rich, delightful slice of nourishment.

Makes: 12 servings | **Prep time:** 15 to 20 minutes | **Set time:** 4 hours

Crust

1 cup almonds

1 cup walnuts

½ teaspoon salt

2 tablespoons coconut oil

4 dates, pitted and torn into pieces

Cashew Cheesecake Top

1⅔ cups soaked cashews, strained and rinsed

1 cup soaked macadamia nuts, strained and rinsed

¼ cup plus 1 tablespoon coconut oil

¼ cup freshly squeezed lemon juice

2 teaspoons lemon zest

¼ cup coconut milk

1½ teaspoons gelatin

1½ teaspoons beet powder

1 tablespoon robust, dark amber maple syrup

2 teaspoon vanilla extract

Toppings

Freeze-dried raspberries

Large coconut shreds

Cacao nibs

1. In a food processor with an "s" blade, pulse the almonds until they are broken into small pieces.

2. Set the processor to continuously run, and add the walnuts.

3. As the walnuts and almonds are mixing, sprinkle in the salt and pour in the coconut oil.

4. Begin to add the date pieces one at time, about 1 date per 30 to 45 seconds, pulsing as needed to break up large pieces.

5. Once the crust forms into a large ball, scrape with a spatula into a pie tin, using your fingertips to spread and press down. Place in the freezer to set for about 10 minutes while making the filling.

6. In a clean food processor with an "s" blade, blend the cashews, macadamia nuts, coconut oil, lemon juice, and lemon zest for about 5 minutes to make a creamy texture while container starts to heat from running motor. Stop to scrape the sides every minute or so.

7. As the ingredients are combining, in a separate small bowl, mix the coconut milk with the gelatin. Allow to sit for about 2 to 3 minutes to bloom.

8. When the desired texture is achieved at the creamy 5-minute mark, add the coconut milk gelatin blend to the processor, blending nonstop for another minute.

9. Add the beet powder, maple syrup, and vanilla and blend for an additional 30 to 45 seconds, stopping to scrape the sides midway. Turn off the processor and scrape the sides once more to gather.

10. Pull the pie crust from the freezer and fill it with the cashew macadamia coconut filling, spreading evenly with a spatula.

11. Cover with parchment or plastic wrap and place in the freezer to set for at least 4 hours, storing up to 2 weeks.

12. Remove the cheesecake and allow to sit at room temperature for about 20 minutes before slicing and serving. Top slices with freeze-dried raspberries, cacao nibs, and coconut shreds.

Note: To soak cashews and macadamia nuts, place in a medium bowl, fill the bowl with water, and allow to soak for 6 to 12 hours at room temperature.

Nutrition facts per serving

Calories: 370 | Carbohydrates: 15g | Fiber: 5g | Protein: 7g | Fat: 34g

Cacao Walnut Fudge

(ef)

FOOD AS MEDICINE   Yes, by now you see that chocolate is medicine and food, not candy, but that comes with a disclaimer. Unfortunately, many chocolate bars out there use processed cocoa, which is very different from cacao as it is heat- and chemical-treated, losing many health-supporting properties. Also, most processed chocolate and cocoa products have additives like soy-based emulsifiers or, worse, TBHQ (tert-Butylhydroquinone), a preservative shown to drive restlessness, hyperventilation, and a sense of delirium—not what we are looking to do here!

Raw cacao powder contains heat-sensitive tryptophan, serotonin, anandamide, the bliss molecule, and phenylethylamine to support a blissful mood. Phenylethylamine is present in the brain during orgasm and seen in high amounts when an individual is in love, supporting optimism, joy, and attraction. It has been proven to alleviate depression. Raw cacao is unique in that it has more bioactive nutrients and neurotransmitters and plays a role as a MAO-inhibitor, a class of antidepressants, ensuring the feel-good signals reach the brain for mood stability.

This recipe is an awesome base for adding other adaptogenic herbs such as ashwagandha to prevent burnout and support stress-induced fatigue. Mucuna purines, which aid in circulating levels of dopamine, are another great option.

Makes: 16 squares | Prep time: 5 to 10 minutes | Set time: 4 to 6 hours

3 cups walnuts, soaked 8 hours, strained, and rinsed

1 cup coconut oil, melted

⅔ cup cacao powder

¼ teaspoon salt

1 teaspoon vanilla extract

¼ cup robust, dark amber maple syrup

¾ teaspoon coarse salt

2 teaspoons cacao nibs

1. In a food processor with an "s" blade, blend the soaked walnuts, coconut oil, cacao powder, salt, vanilla, and maple syrup for 2 minutes, pulsing if needed in the beginning to break down large pieces.

2. Once all of the ingredients are creamy and well combined, stop the processor and, using a rubber spatula, spread them into a glass or metal 10 x 10-inch pan.

3. Sprinkle the coarse salt and cacao nibs on top and set in the freezer for 4 to 6 hours or overnight.

4. Cut into 16 squares and store in the freezer for 2 weeks, if they last that long!

Nutrition per square

Calories: 296 | Carbohydrates: 9g | Fiber: 3g | Protein: 4g | Fat: 28g

Truffled Rosemary Marcona Almonds (ef)

FOOD AS MEDICINE This dish is 100% what I mean when I preach "channel savory" in tackling cravings on the ketogenic diet. The salty, crunchy, umami goodness pairs well with a glass of crisp white wine or robust red wine. It also makes a nice midday snack that crushes stress levels with a boost of oleic acid, shown to decrease anger, enhance mood, and increase energy levels. This snack provides a potent punch of vitamin E to reduce free radical damage and aging while supporting hormone balance. Rosemary is a great anti-inflammatory herb that is often used as a natural preservative due to its antioxidant capacity. This herb may also aid with memory, a welcome midweek food-as-medicine addition.

Makes: 16 servings | **Prep time:** 5 minutes | **Cook time:** 12 to 18 minutes

2½ cups whole raw Marcona almonds

3 tablespoons olive oil

1 tablespoon white truffle extra-virgin olive oil

1 tablespoon minced fresh rosemary

1 tablespoon coarse salt, divided

1. Preheat the oven to 350°F.

2. Place the raw Marcona almonds on an ungreased baking sheet and bake for 5 minutes.

3. While the nuts are in the oven, mix the olive oil, truffle oil, rosemary, and 1 teaspoon of salt in a small bowl.

4. Pull the almonds from the oven and pour the mixture over the nuts. Use a spatula to coat, then return the almonds to the oven for 5 minutes.

5. Toss again and shake the baking sheet, then return to the oven for another 5 to 7 minutes.

6. Remove from the oven when aromatic and slightly brown (too brown will make a bitter burned flavor).

7. Toss the nuts in the remaining 1 to 2 teaspoons of salt and serve warm.

8. Store the remaining nuts at room temperature in an airtight container for up to 1 week.

Nutrition facts per serving

Calories: 137 | **Carbohydrates:** 3g | **Fiber:** 2g | **Protein:** 4g | **Fat:** 13g

Smoothies and Shakes

All too often smoothies are sugar bombs while protein shakes are just a delivery method for processed additives; some of these drinks have over 100 grams of carbs (that's like 7 slices of bread!) and over 10 processed ingredients, including artificial colorants, non-caloric sweeteners, binders, fillers, soy, corn, and protein isolates (not a whole food).

The recipes in this book are made with whole foods, which provide excellent nutrient density. The drinks are also an easy way for children to get in greens, brain-boosting fats, and other antioxidant-rich nutrients. You can throw together these smoothies and shakes in a snap for on-the-go mornings, post-workout recovery drinks, meal replacements, or an awesome way to get greens in when you just don't have time to chew!

For these recipes, blend in the protein after all the other ingredients are well incorporated, especially when using non-denatured grass-fed whey. Good-quality whey, such as my *Naturally Nourished Grassfed Whey*, does not have binders or fillers for added weight, which can produce an undesired frothy head if blended too soon in the mixing process.

What Is Collagen and Why Is It Recommended?

Collagen peptides are derived from beef hide in bovine sources as well as fish skin or scales in marine sources. Collagen aids in connective tissue formation, which supports hair, skin, and nail health, as well as bone, joint, and tendon function and repair. Beyond structural health, collagen tightens gut junctions to aid in repair from leaky gut while supporting improved ability to absorb nutrients. The amino acid profile of collagen is rich in glycine and proline, which balance out consumption of meat products (especially ground meat) high in methionine that can hinder detoxification pathways and methylation activity, driving inflammatory processes. Glycine also helps the body metabolize fat and provides support as an anxiolytic with neuromuscular relaxation and promotion of GABA expression.

These shakes can be modified for children or those who aren't participating in a ketogenic diet. To do so, blend in a 3-inch piece of frozen banana, 1 pitted date, or ½ cup of additional frozen fruit. These shakes and smoothies are developed to provide protein as a meal replacement option, but if you are using them as a snack, you may omit the protein and consume a half portion, if desired.

Below is a helpful matrix to aid in your own recipe creations with ingredients you have on hand.

FAT: 1 to 3 choices	+	LIQUID: ½ to 1 cup	+	FOOD AS MEDICINE BOOSTS: 1 to 2 choices	+	PROTEIN (optional): 15 to 30 grams
• 1 tablespoon nut butter (pecan, almond, macadamia, Brazil) • 2 teaspoons coconut butter • ¼ cup full-fat coconut milk • 2 to 8 nuts of choice • 1 tablespoon chia or flax seed • ¼ avocado, with 1 teaspoon coconut oil		• water • coconut water • unsweetened almond or nut milk of choice (no binders or fillers) • coconut milk (this counts as a fat as well) • cold-brew coffee • ice as desired		• kale • spinach • swiss chard • fresh or ground ginger • fresh or ground turmeric • basil • cacao powder or nibs • matcha green tea powder • lime • lemon • cinnamon • maca powder		• 1 to 2 scoops grass-fed whey • 2 to 4 scoops collagen peptides • ½ to 1 cup full-fat Greek yogurt

Directions

All shakes and smoothies take about 5 to 10 minutes to make, including cleanup! To make, add all ingredients except protein powder to a blender and mix on high speed. Once the ingredients are smooth and well combined, whip in the protein for a couple seconds to incorporate..

Why Consider Whey, Isn't That Dairy?

Grass-fed whey's protein bioavailability is high, which means it's easy to absorb and a majority of its protein is used directly by your body. You'll find amino acids such as glutamine (good for gut restoration) and asparagine (good for the nervous system and immune support). In dairy, whey is the opposing protein to casein, so a quality sourced and extracted whey (such as Naturally Nourished Grassfed Whey Protein) should be free of casein and lactose as well as low-heat processed or non-denatured. This maintains the active immunoglobulins and antioxidants such as glutathione, which actually reduces inflammation. If you're not sure that you can tolerate dairy, eliminate all forms for the first 12 weeks; however, you may consider bringing back ghee and grass-fed whey in week 7.

Almond Butter Berry Smoothie
(ef)

Makes: 2 (1-cup) servings

⅓ cup frozen grapes

¼ cup frozen blueberries

1½ cups unsweetened almond milk

3 tablespoons almond butter, fresh ground is best

1 scoop Naturally Nourished Grassfed Whey Protein or 2 scoops collagen peptides (16 grams)

Nutrition facts per serving
Calories: 373 | Carbohydrates: 16g | Fiber: 4g | Protein: 31g | Fat: 23g

Matcha Blueberry Green Smoothie
(nf) (ef)

Makes: 1 (1½-cup) serving

½ teaspoon matcha tea powder

⅓ cup full-fat coconut milk

⅓ cup filtered water

⅓ cup frozen blueberries

1 teaspoon lemon zest

1 tablespoon lemon juice

2 cups leafy greens

1 scoop Naturally Nourished Grassfed Whey Protein or 2 scoops collagen peptides (16 grams)

Nutrition facts per serving
Calories: 306 | Carbohydrates: 15g | Fiber: 4g | Protein: 26g | Fat: 16g

Berry Cream Smoothie

(nf) (ef)

Makes: 1 (1-cup) serving

1 cup frozen strawberries

½ cup frozen raspberries

⅓ cup full-fat coconut milk

1 tablespoon lemon juice

1 scoop Naturally Nourished Grassfed Whey Protein or 2 scoops collagen peptides (16 grams)

Nutrition facts per serving
Calories: 301 | Carbohydrates: 15g | Fiber: 4g | Protein: 25g | Fat: 16g

Avocado Green Smoothie

(ef)

Makes: 2 (1-cup) servings

¾ cup full-fat coconut milk

¾ cup water

2 tablespoons macadamia nuts

½ inch fresh ginger

juice of ½ lime

2 cups leafy greens of choice, the darker the better

½ avocado, cubed

1 cup ice

1½ scoops Naturally Nourished Grassfed Whey Protein or 3 scoops collagen peptides (24 grams)

Nutrition facts per serving
Calories: 372 | Carbohydrates: 13g | Fiber: 5g | Protein: 21g | Fat: 27g

Keto Citrus Burst Smoothie

(nf) (ef)

Makes: 2 (1¼-cup) servings

½ cup frozen mango

½ cup frozen raspberries

½ orange, peeled

1 tablespoon lemon juice

⅔ cup full-fat coconut milk

½ cup water

2 tablespoons hemp seeds

1 inch turmeric root

1 scoop Naturally Nourished Grassfed Whey Protein or 2 scoops collagen peptides (16 grams)

Nutrition facts per serving
Calories: 316 | Carbohydrates: 17g | Fiber: 4g | Protein: 17g | Fat: 20g

ABC Shake (Almond Butter and Chocolate)

(ef)

Makes: 1 (¾-cup) serving

¾ cup unsweetened almond milk

1 tablespoon almond butter

1 tablespoon raw cacao powder

1 teaspoon vanilla extract

1 scoop Naturally Nourished Grassfed Whey Protein or 2 scoops collagen peptides (16 grams)

Nutrition facts per serving
Calories: 245 | Carbohydrates: 9g | Fiber: 2g | Protein: 29g | Fat: 12g

Simple Cinnamon Almond Shake

(ef)

Makes: 1 (1½-cup) serving

1 tablespoon almond butter

1 teaspoon vanilla extract

¼ teaspoon ground cinnamon

1 cup unsweetened almond milk

2 to 3 ice cubes

1 scoop Naturally Nourished Grassfed Whey Protein or 2 scoops collagen peptides (16 grams)

Nutrition facts per serving
Calories: 338 | Carbohydrates: 11g |
Fiber: 3g | Protein: 31g | Fat: 21g

Cacao Coconut Cashew Shake

(ef)

Makes: 1 (1½-cup) serving

2 cups cashew milk

2 tablespoons coconut butter

1½ tablespoons raw cacao powder

2 tablespoons large coconut flakes

1 tablespoon maca powder

½ avocado

1 date

pinch of salt

Nutrition facts per serving
Calories: 370 | Carbohydrates: 23g |
Fiber: 9g | Protein: 20g | Fat: 23g

Almond Collagen Hot Cocoa (ef)

FOOD AS MEDICINE This hot chocolate has the decadent taste of a peanut butter cup with an upgrade to almond butter, without all of the artificial flavors and preservatives. When choosing a chocolate bar, always look for one with at least 80% cacao, but when you are using raw cacao powder you are getting 100% pure cacao. The antioxidants in cacao exceed red wine and even green tea. Cacao is high in magnesium, which can help lower blood pressure and relax muscles; it also provides theobromine, a bitter alkaloid that supports healthy serotonin levels. The addition of collagen supports a balanced carb-to-protein ratio while providing gut, hair, skin, and nail support.

Makes: 2 (1-cup) servings | **Prep time:** 5 minutes | **Cook time:** 10 to 15 minutes

1 cup full-fat coconut milk

½ cup filtered water

3 tablespoons raw cacao powder

2 tablespoons almond butter

1 date, pitted

2 teaspoons vanilla extract

¼ teaspoon sea salt

2 scoops collagen peptides (16 grams)

1. Heat the coconut milk and water on low until it simmers, then slowly whisk in the cacao and almond butter until well combined.

2. Remove from the heat. Add to a blender along with the date, vanilla, and sea salt.

3. Blend on high for 45 to 60 seconds until well incorporated.

4. Add the collagen and mix again for about 15 to 30 seconds. Pour into 2 mugs.

Nutrition facts per serving

Calories: 374 | Carbohydrates: 11g | Fiber: 3g | Protein: 12g | Fat: 30g

Nut Milk: A Source of Nutrient Density or Thickened Water?

Due to rising levels of dairy intolerance, many people are choosing nut milks as their go-to base in lattes, smoothies, and protein shakes. This transition reduces the consumption of casein, the inflammatory compound in dairy that can cross the blood-brain barrier and interfere with opioid receptors that influence mood and behavior; however, many nut milks are glorified water at best. Most nut milks have stabilizers like carrageenan, known to cause gut-lining damage and, potentially, cancer. Adding insult to injury, dairy-free milks are often synthetically enriched with poor-quality vitamins and minerals that may drive more imbalance. Just don't do it!

Use water in your shakes and smoothies and add 1 to 2 tablespoons of nut butter for every 6 to 8 ounces of water. Blend on high to get more nutrient density and make "lazy man's nut milk" with no straining required. Or, follow the timeline below to soak nuts, using a ratio of ⅓ cup of nuts to ⅔ cup of water per desired thickness. Then, follow the instructions in Pistachio Golden Milk (page 134) or Macadamia Brazil Nut Milk (page 133). I like to add 1 to 2 dates for mouthfeel and as a natural thickener and sweetener. Don't forget that pinch of salt to provide a nice flavor bridge while supporting electrolytes.

Why Soak Your Nuts?

Nuts have many anti-nutrients that inhibit digestive enzymes, driving bloating and digestive distress while blocking the ability to absorb nutrients. Soaking your nuts based on fat concentration will aid in mimicking the germination process, reducing the phytic acid and other anti-nutrient compounds, so the plant releases its defense mechanisms and prepares for growth with a surge of nutrient density. You may consider adding 1 teaspoon of lemon juice or Bragg Apple Cider Vinegar to enhance the breakdown process and further aid in nutrient absorption.

Fat Level	Nut	Soak time
High-fat nuts	Macadamia nuts, pine nuts, cashews	Soak for 2 to 4 hours
Medium-fat nuts	Brazil nuts, pecans, walnuts	Soak for 4 to 8 hours
Lower-fat, higher-fiber nuts	Almonds, pistachios, hazelnuts	Soak for 8 to 12 hours

Macadamia Brazil Nut Milk (ef)

FOOD AS MEDICINE This high-fat nut milk supports your ketogenic diet and hormone rebound while providing satiety and metabolic support. Macadamia nuts are rich in monounsaturated fats and tocotrienols that support cognitive health and mood while protecting the brain from oxidative stress. The Brazil nuts provide a rich source of selenium, which aids in metabolic support and thyroid function. Selenium reduces toxins in the body and reduces inflammation in the thyroid gland. It also aids in the conversion of inactive hormone T4 to active form T3 while helping the body efficiently recycle iodine.

Makes: 4 (12-ounce) servings | **Prep time:** 15 minutes plus 3 to 4 hours soak time

2 cups raw macadamia nuts

1 cup Brazil nuts

5 cups filtered water

2 dates

pinch of salt (about ⅛ teaspoon)

1 teaspoon vanilla extract (optional)

1. Place the macadamia and Brazil nuts in a large bowl and add enough water to completely cover.

2. Soak for 3 to 4 hours, then strain and rinse the nuts. Discard the soaking water, which gets rid of phytates and anti-nutrients.

3. Add nuts to a blender along with the filtered water. Blend on high for 3 minutes.

4. Pour the mixture through a nut bag or strainer into a large bowl.

5. Return the strained nut milk to the blender and add the dates, salt, and vanilla, if using. Blend on high for another 2 minutes.

6. Serve warm just out of the blender or store in a glass jar in the refrigerator for up to 5 days.

Nutrition facts per serving

Calories: 447 | Carbohydrates: 10g | Fiber: 3g | Protein: 6g | Fat: 45g

Pistachio Golden Milk

(ef)

FOOD AS MEDICINE   With ancient origins in India, this health-promoting beverage supports immune health, reduces inflammation, and balances hormones. Rather than a base of cow's or coconut milk, which can be too reminiscent of a curry dish, the recipe uses pistachio milk to provide a robust nutty flavor and a boost of pyridoxine (vitamin B6) to support neurotransmitter conversion and promote deep, restful sleep. A touch of maple helps tryptophan, the building block for serotonin, cross more easily into the brain for use. Serotonin is the precursor to melatonin, the powerful antioxidant that aids in depth and quality of sleep. With ginger and cayenne, this drink can be a fitting start to the day but may be best to sip deeply when practicing relaxation techniques.

Makes: 1 (16-ounce) serving | Prep time: 5 minutes

2 cups pistachio milk (see recipe below)

1 teaspoon ground turmeric

¼ teaspoon ground cinnamon

⅛ teaspoon ground ginger

1 teaspoon robust, dark maple syrup

1 tablespoon coconut oil

pinch of salt

pinch of cayenne pepper

pinch of freshly ground black pepper

Add all the ingredients to a blender and blend on high for about 1 minute.

Nutrition facts per serving

Calories: 206 | Carbohydrates: 7g | Fiber: 1g | Protein: 2g | Fat: 19g

How to Make Pistachio Milk

If you can't find pistachio milk, it's easy to make your own. Soak 1 cup raw, unsalted shelled pistachios in water for 8 to 12 hours. Rinse and drain, discarding the soaking water. Place the soaked pistachios in a blender with 3 cups filtered water and blend until smooth, about 2 minutes. Add ½ date and blend on high until combined, another 2 minutes. Pour the contents of the blender through a nut milk bag into a jar with a lid. Store in the refrigerator for 4 to 5 days. Be sure to shake before using as water may separate.

Anti-Inflammatory Electrolyte Elixir (nf) (ef)

FOOD AS MEDICINE   This recipe provides the anti-inflammatory benefits of turmeric while stabilizing electrolytes as you transition into ketosis or a lower-carbohydrate diet. It also makes a great post-workout recovery beverage and supports the adrenals as vitamin C is most concentrated in this tiny stress gland.

Makes: 6 (8-ounce) servings | **Prep time:** 10 minutes

2 inches turmeric root, peeled and chopped

3 lemons, peeled, with white pith intact

5 cups filtered water

1 cup unsweetened coconut water

½ to 1 teaspoon salt

Blend all of the ingredients in a blender until completely broken down, about 1 minute on high. If desired, strain for a smoother texture and discard the pulp. Place in a mason jar and shake well to incorporate. Serve on ice or store in the refrigerator for up to 1 week.

Nutrition facts per serving

Calories: 11 | **Carbohydrates:** 3g | **Fiber:** 0g | **Protein:** 0g | **Fat:** 0g

Chapter 10

Therapeutics/ Condiments

Bacteria-Battling Chimichurri (nf) (ef)

Makes: 6 (2-tablespoon) servings | Prep time: 10 to 15 minutes

¼ cup fresh parsley leaves

¼ cup fresh basil leaves

2 tablespoons fresh oregano

5 cloves garlic, smashed

2 tablespoons lemon juice (juice of 1 lemon)*

½ cup unrefined, extra-virgin olive oil

2 teaspoons sea salt, plus more to taste

¼ teaspoon white pepper

2 teaspoons red chili flakes

1. In a food processor with an "s" blade, combine the first five ingredients on high.

2. After a minute or so, use a spatula to scrape the sides, and mix again for a minute.

3. Scrape the sides again, then, while the machine is running, pour in the olive oil at a constant drizzle. Then sprinkle in the salt, pepper, and chili flakes.

4. Adjust the flavors to taste, adding additional salt as needed.

If you are doing vinegar at this time and not during the first 3 weeks of a candida cleanse, try substituting 1 tablespoon Bragg Apple Cider Vinegar for half the lemon juice to benefit from the probiotic yeast strains.

Nutrition facts per serving

Calories: 170 | Carbohydrates: 2g | Fiber: 1g | Protein: 1g | Fat: 18g

MCT Oil Ketchup (nf)(ef)

Makes: 8 (2-tablespoon) servings | Prep time: 5 minutes

1 (6-ounce) jar tomato paste

3 tablespoons MCT oil

2 tablespoons apple cider vinegar

¼ teaspoon onion granules

¼ teaspoon garlic powder

¼ teaspoon white pepper

¾ teaspoon salt

½ teaspoon robust, dark amber maple syrup

1. In a large bowl with a whisk or in a blender, add all ingredients and combine until well blended.

2. Store in an airtight jar in the fridge for 2 to 3 weeks.

Nutrition facts per serving

Calories: 72 | Carbohydrates: 5g | Fiber: 1g | Protein: 2g | Fat: 5g

What Is MCT Oil?

Medium-chain triglycerides (MCT) are fatty acids found in tropical oils such as coconut and palm oil, as well as isolated into MCT oil formulas. Due to their unique smaller size, MCTs are easily digested without requiring bile, making them a great choice for those on a high-fat ketogenic diet while struggling with liver or gallbladder issues. MCTs are also able to cross directly into the mitochondria, the energy factories within each cell in our body, providing a boost of energy and brain support while supporting ketone production. Adding MCT oil to children's condiments (and yours) or even in fruits can be a great way to support blood sugar balance and provide the benefits of ketones. I am a big fan of coconut oil as a whole-food source of MCTs; however, a quality MCT oil product can be very versatile and is free of coconut flavor.

Simple Kale Pesto

(ef)

Makes: 4 (⅛-cup) servings | **Prep time:** 5 to 10 minutes

large bunch basil, stemmed (about ¼ packed cup)

½ cup lacinato kale, stemmed and chopped

½ teaspoon salt

juice of 1 lemon (about ⅛ cup)

¼ cup pine nuts

¼ cup olive oil

1. In a blender or food processor with an "s" blade, combine basil, kale, salt, and lemon.

2. Once the ingredients are combined, pulse in the pine nuts to incorporate, following by the olive oil drizzled at a steady stream with the motor running to emulsify.

3. Serve immediately or store in an airtight glass jar in the fridge for 3 to 5 days.

Nutrition facts per serving

Calories: 132 | Carbohydrates: 2g | Fiber: 1g | Protein: 0g | Fat: 14g

Caramelized Onions

(nf)(ef)

Makes: 6 (¼-cup) servings | **Prep time:** 5 minutes | **Cook time:** 12 to 15 minutes

1 tablespoon coconut oil

2 yellow onions, thinly sliced (about 3 cups)

½ teaspoon salt

1. Heat a cast-iron pan over medium-high heat. Add the coconut oil and onion.

2. Stir to coat the pieces and let sit for 3 minutes. Then, stir again for about 30 seconds and allow to sit for another 3 minutes.

3. Do this 2 more times, adding sprinkles of salt in between for about 10 to12 minutes total until onions are soft and brown, and some pieces are crispy.

Nutrition facts per serving

Calories: 30 | Carbohydrates: 2g | Fiber: 1g | Protein: 0g | Fat: 2g

Avocado Hollandaise

(nf) (ef)

Makes: 4 (⅛-cup) servings | **Prep time:** 5 to 10 minutes

1 large ripe avocado, pitted

2 tablespoons freshly squeezed lemon juice

¼ cup full-fat coconut milk

⅛ cup water

4 to 5 basil leaves

¼ teaspoon sea salt, to taste

⅛ teaspoon ground white pepper

pinch of cayenne pepper

1. In a blender, blend together the avocado, lemon juice, coconut milk, and water until combined into a creamy base.

2. Add the remaining ingredients to the blender and mix on high until well incorporated.

3. Serve immediately or store in an airtight glass jar in the fridge for 3 to 4 days.

Nutrition facts per serving

Calories: 84 | Carbohydrates: 5g | Fiber: 3g | Protein: 1g | Fat: 8g

Herbed Lemon Salad Dressing

(nf) (ef)

Makes: 2 (2-tablespoon) servings | **Prep time:** 5 minutes

1 tablespoon chopped fresh flat Italian parsley

2 tablespoons chopped fresh basil

1 tablespoon lemon juice

1 tablespoon red wine vinegar

2 tablespoons olive oil

½ teaspoon mustard

5 cracks freshly ground black pepper

generous pinch of salt

1. In a medium bowl, add all of the ingredients and whisk to incorporate.

2. Serve immediately or store in an airtight glass jar at room temperature for 3 to 5 days.

Nutrition facts per serving

Calories: 126 | Carbohydrates: 1g | Fiber: 0g | Protein: 0g | Fat: 14g

Rustic Balsamic Dressing

Makes: 6 (3-tablespoon) servings | Prep time: 5 minutes

½ cup balsamic vinegar

½ cup olive oil

1 tablespoon mustard

1 tablespoon robust, dark amber maple syrup

1 teaspoon garlic, minced (about 2 cloves)

1 tablespoon chopped fresh rosemary

1 tablespoon chopped fresh oregano

2 teaspoons fresh thyme leaves

½ teaspoon salt

½ teaspoon freshly ground black pepper

1. Place all of the ingredients in a jar with a tight-fitting lid and shake vigorously for 2 to 3 minutes.

2. Serve immediately or store at room temperature for 5 to 7 days. Shake again briefly prior to serving.

Nutrition facts per serving

Calories: 192 | Carbohydrates: 6g | Fiber: 0g | Protein: 0g | Fat: 18g

Golden Lemon Zinger Dressing

Makes: 8 (2½-tablespoon) servings | Prep time: 5 minutes

1 tablespoon chopped fresh turmeric

1 teaspoon chopped fresh ginger

½ cup fresh lemon juice (about 3 lemons)

½ teaspoon salt

1 teaspoon raw honey

¼ teaspoon freshly ground black pepper

1 tablespoon champagne vinegar

⅔ cup olive oil

1. Blend all of the ingredients except for the olive oil in a blender on medium, pulsing to break up the chopped roots. Increase speed to high until well combined and getting creamy, adding an additional teaspoon of water at a time as needed.

2. Once incorporated and desired texture is achieved, drizzle in olive oil while motor is running to emulsify and create an even creamier texture.

3. Serve immediately, storing leftovers in a mason jar at room temperature for 4 to 5 days.

Nutrition facts per serving

Calories: 171 | Carbohydrates: 3g | Fiber: 0g | Protein: 0g | Fat: 18g

Mellow Mama Dressing

(nf) (ef)

Makes: 6 (2-tablespoon) servings | **Prep time: 5 minutes**

2 tablespoons chopped fresh basil

2 cloves garlic, smashed

¼ cup tahini

¼ avocado

⅓ cup lemon juice

1 tablespoon organic raw unfiltered apple cider vinegar

2 tablespoons fresh chopped rosemary

1 teaspoon sea salt

2 tablespoons water, plus more as needed to thin

3 tablespoons olive oil

1. Blend all of the ingredients except for the olive oil in blender. Increase speed to high until well combined and getting creamy, adding an additional teaspoon of water as needed.

2. Once incorporated and desired texture is achieved, drizzle in olive oil while motor is running to emulsify and create an even creamier texture.

3. Once blended, add additional teaspoons of water if needed to achieve desired texture.

4. Serve immediately, storing leftovers in a mason jar in the fridge for 5 to 7 days.

Note: This recipe can be kept thicker to use as a dip.

Nutrition facts per serving

Calories: 184 | **Carbohydrates:** 4g | **Fiber:** 2g | **Protein:** 5g | **Fat** 17g

Elderberry Gummies

(nf) (ef)

FOOD AS MEDICINE Elderberry is one of the top antiviral herbs on the planet and can aid in reducing cold and flu symptoms, as well as nerve pain, inflammation, allergies, and sinus issues. The addition of vitamin C from the lemon and orange helps fight infection as well, and the gelatin in this recipe is very therapeutic for the lining of the gut.

Makes: 12 gummies | Prep Time: 10 minutes | Set time: 4 to 6 hours

2 tablespoons Further Food Beef Gelatin

½ cup water, room temperature or warm

¾ cup fresh-squeezed orange juice

3 tablespoons fresh-squeezed lemon juice

2 tablespoons elderberry syrup

1. In a small bowl, bloom the gelatin in the water by whisking with a fork until dissolved, then allowing it to sit for about 5 minutes.

2. In a medium saucepan, heat the orange juice, lemon juice, and elderberry syrup, stirring to combine and heat through.

3. Once the gelatin has sat for 5 minutes, pour it into the hot simmering liquid. Turn off the heat but stir continuously for about 30 to 45 seconds.

4. Pour the liquid into a glass pan or silicone molds and set for 4 to 6 hours in the fridge.

5. If in glass pan, cut into cubes and, if in molds, pop out prior to eating!

Nutrition facts per gummy

Calories: 26 | Carbohydrates: 2g | Fiber: 0g | Protein: 2g | Fat: 0g

Coconut Fruit Constipation Puree (nf)(ef)

FOOD AS MEDICINE Prunes and apricots are well known as a remedy for constipation thanks to their high fiber content, especially insoluble fiber to fuel healthy gut bacteria. Prunes help soften stool, increase bowel movement frequency, and decrease digestive pain. I always say, however, that too much fiber without adequate water can act like a brick instead of a broom! This puree includes coconut oil to aid in lubrication of the bowels and can be taken as a tea to increase fluid consumption and manage dehydration, a very common cause of constipation in the first place! Apricots can be subbed for prunes in this recipe and will yield similar results!

Makes: 6 (2-tablespoon) servings | Prep time: 5 to 10 minutes

½ cup dried prunes or apricots, soaked in warm water for about 1 hour

½ cup extra virgin coconut oil, melted

¼ cup room-temperature lemon juice

¼ teaspoon Himalayan pink salt

1 tablespoon honey (optional)

1. Strain the soaked fruit and reserve the water; you may use the water to thin the puree if desired.

2. In a blender or food processor, mix the melted coconut oil with the lemon juice, fruit, salt, and optional honey, pulsing to create a nice creamy puree and adding soaking water 1 teaspoon at a time, as needed.

3. Once all of the ingredients are well incorporated, store in a mason jar to have 1 serving daily, adding 2 tablespoons to heated water like a tea.

4. You may also eat with a spoon in 2- to 3-tablespoon portions and then follow up with 16 ounces of room-temperature water.

Nutrition facts per serving

Calories: 196 | Carbohydrates: 9g | Fiber: 3g | Protein: 0g | Fat: 16g

Acknowledgments

To my anti-anxiety diet real food warriors: May you find hope and direction with a pathway toward mental clarity, improved mood, and a mellow state of mind. Keep pushing and working to honor your body with your intake. You are worth it!

With crazy love and gratitude to:

- Brady, my husband and cornerstone, who grounds my energy always with a lightness through the hustle, belly laughing along the way. He does ALL the things in my company and in our household, allowing me to keep pushing my passion. You are my everything, Mr. Miller.

- Stella, my daughter, who makes living in the moment very real and shows me daily how to find my breath. Being your mama is the greatest gift and I am so grateful to support your journey in this beautiful place.

- Becki Yoo, RD, LD, my work wife, who took all the beautiful photography to bring this book to life! She keeps it rocking with weekly content blogs and media as an authentic extension of the Ali Miller, RD, brand. She is a skilled practitioner, dynamic podcast cohost, and amazing friend.

- My family, thank you for always supporting me even when I pushed outside the box, believing in me and allowing me to grow.

About the Author

Ali Miller, RD, LD, CDE, is a registered dietitian with a naturopathic background and a contagious passion for using nutrients and food as the foundation of treatment protocols and programs. Her food-as-medicine philosophy is supported by up-to-date scientific research for a functional integrative approach to healing the body. Ali is a certified diabetes educator (CDE) and renowned expert in the ketogenic diet, with over a decade of clinical results using a unique whole-foods approach tailored to support thyroid, adrenal, and hormonal balance. Ali's message has influenced millions in the medical community and media with television, print, and her award-winning podcast, Naturally Nourished. Ali's website, www.alimillerrd.com, offers her blog, podcasts, virtual learning, and access to her practice and supplement line Naturally Nourished.